Gay Priest

&

The Woman
Who Loves Her

The Pain and Promise
of a Gay Marriage

Karen B. Hunter

A WICWAS BOOK

ISBN:1-878075-16-0
© 2004 by Karen B. Hunter
All Rights Reserved
Printed in the United States of America
Published by Wicwas Press, LLC
New Haven, Connecticut 06515
United States of America

First Edition

Book design and new artwork by Larry Connor
Cover photo provided by the author.

Dedication

This book is for the children,
with a special dedication to the eldest grandchild
who has carried the greatest burden,
and the youngest, whom we hope someday to meet.

Contents

Acknowledgments

First, any aptitude I have with words comes directly from my parents who are both fine writers. For every sentence that is verbally correct I must credit my father, for whom a misplaced adverb or spoken redundancy (to "commute back and forth" or go around a "rotary circle," for example) were greater cause for concern when I was a child than, say, a baseball thrown through the front-hall window. For a deep understanding of hospitality and a core sense of good manners—no small thing these days—I credit my mother. About my daughters—two of the most fascinating people I know and of whom I am completely in awe—I can only acknowledge with wonder the gift of their unconditional love.

For research questions as I began this project, I thank Jill Huie and Cathy Ahern, my *de-facto* "librarians-in-residence," for their enthusiasm and quick responses day or night. For computer crisis management, I am forever indebted to Liz Trynosky, without whose intervention we might not be having this conversation.

For editing, it was my great good fortune to have the best. I am *eternally grateful* to the following: Linda Stanley, of Stanley Communications, who read my first tentative chapters, gave powerful feedback, convinced me to write chapters I never would have thought of, and stood strong in a stance of encouragement ("You *must* keep going; you *must* get this published!"). Marta Daniels, author and peace activist, among many other things, who is a sleuth when it comes to faulty grammar, sloppy transitions, and missing links and who quietly and firmly pointed out exactly what needed to be "fixed" after each reading. My stepfather, Fred Stocking, Morris Professor of Rhetoric Emeritus at Williams College, whose frank, eloquent, and utterly on-target written comments after thorough readings of the manuscript (particularly on points of ambiguous language) are themselves worthy of publication. I had to admit—after he removed ninety percent of my commas, half of the semicolons, and added some exclamation points—that he was right on *almost* all counts (!).

For proofreading, the last frontier of any publishing project and an area which requires a razor-sharp aptitude few possess, I give full credit to Leah Ann Portley, courageous daughter-in-law of the priest and partner-in-crime to me in the in-law department.

Special mention and gratitude go to the Most Rev. Lorraine Bouffard of the Ecumenical Catholic Church, for inviting me to her Tuesday evening book group where I was introduced to the lucid and prophetic writings of Marcus Borg, Richard Holloway, and John Shelby Spong, and through whom I have had the great privilege of meeting in person two of the three of these brilliant men; to Frank O'Gorman of *People of Faith for Gay Civil Rights* for his news updates on homosexuality-related issues via email; and to Larry Connor of Wicwas Press, our "brother in arms" whose creative suggestions and enthusiasm about publishing this book kept me going all the way to the end.

On the home front I acknowledge Chuck Shepard, whose gift of the land on which we live is, in a way, where this story begins and ends. I acknowledge with gratitude the emotional support of the Active Contemplatives of the

Sanctuary (ACTS), in whose presence (Saturday morning after Saturday morning) I talked about "my book" as they listened without any visible hint of boredom. I acknowledge Rosemary Poole, who has supported me in too many ways to mention here, but above all, who listened with pure focus to readings and re-readings of my book-in-progress for over a year when she had much more important things to do!

Finally, I acknowledge my beautiful partner, "the alpha and omega of Patricias," who is, forever more, the story of my life.

The Gaps

Ezekiel excoriates false prophets as those who have 'not gone up into the gaps.'

The gaps are the thing.

The gaps are the spirit's one home, the altitudes and latitudes so dazzlingly spare and clean that the spirit can discover itself for the first time like a once blind man unbound.

The gaps are the clefts in the rock where you cower to see the back parts of God;

they are the fissures between mountains and cells the wind lances through, the icy narrowing fiords splitting the cliffs of mystery.

Go up into the gaps.

If you can find them; they shift and vanish too.

—Annie Dillard, *Pilgrim at Tinker's Creek*

Forward

There is no personal virtue in me other than this—that I followed a path all may travel but on which few do journey. It is a path within ourselves where the feet first falter in shadow and darkness but which is later made gay by heavenly light.

—*The Candle of Vision*, Parabola Magazine.

This is a book about two lesbians who fell in love and now live in committed relationship. It is also about so much else that to call this a "lesbian book" would limit the nature of its story as severely as calling God "Father" limits the nature and expression of divinity.

When I started writing, America had yet to go to war with Iraq, an openly-gay priest had yet to be elected Bishop of New Hampshire, the country had yet to see same-gender couples by the thousands lining up at town halls to apply for marriage licenses, and the "gay issue" within the Episcopal Church was focused upon the new Archbishop of Canterbury who was about to be *enthroned*. Protestors took to the streets in England, some wearing black arm bands, for the Archbishop-elect had once ordained a "practicing gay man" and had stated that he could *see a cause* for acknowledging faithful same-sex relationships. He did not believe that homosexuality is a sin. The Anglican Church began to implode, and the rest is making history as we speak.

My partner is an Episcopal priest. We follow church news with great interest. I didn't start writing, however, solely because one of us is an Episcopal priest at a time when the Church is in its greatest crisis since the ordination of women; nor because we have decided to live "out loud" as a lesbian couple and can't resist talking about it, nor simply to present ourselves as role models to the people who need role models ("By God, if a priest can come out, so can I!"). All of these are true, but the bottom line is that far too many of us are still in hiding, afraid to talk, afraid to tell. Our stories need to be told until the shame, and the hiding, are over.

My partner's name is the Rev. Patricia Gallagher. She is the public person, the "people" person, the one everyone knows and remembers—the most openly-gay priest in the Episcopal diocese of Connecticut (at the time of this writing), the one "out front on the bicycle with the red flag," as the current bishop has described her. I am the introvert who has made an art of working behind the scenes. Until now, when I surprise myself by taking the risk of going public: I am the woman who loves the gay priest.

This is the story of our lives, our search for spiritual meaning, our relationships with our families, and the politics of the Church. Our story is the microcosm set within a macrocosm that is rapidly unfolding and long overdue. In many ways, except the part about the priest, our story could be any gay couple's story. The "I's" refer to me; the "she's" refer to her. May you find truth and even inspiration within these pages. May we make the world a saner place, one story at a time.

—Karen B. Hunter
East Haddam, Connecticut
Summer, 2004

The Wedding

This is love: to fly toward a secret sky,
To cause a hundred veils to fall
*   each moment*
First to let go of life,
Finally, to take a step without feet.

—Rumi

A year before our Holy Union. The March on Washington, spring of the year 2000. Eight hundred *thousand* of us under bright blue skies and burning hot sun marching, chanting, singing, praying. We want the right to be accepted as who we are. We want to be seen and heard.

Rev. Troy Perry of the Universal Fellowship of Metropolitan Community Churches is presiding over a "mass wedding" for gay couples which he is calling The Wedding. Mass weddings remind me of the "Moonies" and cults. I have no interest. Then we hear that for a $25 fee each couple will be registered and receive a certificate of participation and their names will be placed somewhere in the National Archives. This we should do, I say. The more of us who are registered, the more forcefully we make the point that we, too, want to marry one another and live our lives as committed and legally recognized couples.

This will be a political formality, I think. How sacred could it be to stand with a "mass" of humanity to pledge our love for one another? How meaningful, if not surrounded by close friends and family in an intimate setting? On our way to the steps of the Lincoln Memorial we are interviewed for a documentary, which makes us almost late.

Not to worry, I think, there won't be more than fifty or a hundred of us at the most, and standing room will be easy to find.

Nothing could have prepared me for the hundreds and hundreds of people we joined on those steps at the nation's capitol. Nothing could have taught me more about what happens when the oppressed come together—the sense of solidarity and protectiveness, the respect and courtesy we extend to one another no matter how different we are, the light that shines in our eyes and bursts from our hearts because the day is ours and we're together, and "out," and—for the moment—safe.

Shoulder to shoulder we stand, finding our footing and quieting down. We are so many beautiful people in love. Rev. Perry starts the service, asking us to face our partners and hold one another's hands. He asks us to lean forward and tell our partners why we want to marry them. I lean toward Pat and the "masses" disappear; they aren't "masses" at all—they *are* close friends and family, and this *is* an intimate setting. I don't cry at weddings, mine or anyone else's, but at this moment there are so many tears I can hardly speak.

I want to marry you because you're my beautiful, beautiful woman. We kiss, and someone takes the picture that eventually makes its way to the cover of this book.

Baptism by Fire

By the time we were living together, Pat had baptized all four of her grandchildren. Each ceremony had been, for her, a privilege that went beyond words—welcoming her "babies" into the Kingdom of God through the ritual and Sacrament of Holy Baptism.

The fifth child to be baptized was born when our relationship was new enough that some of the family was still tenuous about it, to use a stark understatement. With this new baby's family, however, we were on civil terms—cordial even. We wondered about the baptism. Pat knew she wouldn't be asked to perform the ceremony out of respect for her ex-husband (seeing her in a public role at a family event so soon after the divorce might be more than he could tolerate) but that's all she knew. Perhaps they were going to have the baby baptized into the father's church, which was a different denomination. Time went on; the baby was almost six months old, and no one was talking to us about a baptism. Finally, Pat decided to ask: "When are you going to have this baby baptized?" Dead silence. Frantic glances at one another. More silence. "We already have," came the answer.

Could they possibly have thought that if they didn't mention it, the subject would simply never come up? Could they possibly have thought that a priest, who had baptized every one of her first four grandchildren, would simply *not notice* if the baptism of the fifth was never discussed? This shattering omission forced Pat to wrestle with something no one had had the guts to admit, and which she found hard to believe (these are her *children*, she kept tell-ing herself): that when push came to shove, even when life was looking fairly normal, even for those within the family who said they loved her and had "no problem" with the homosexual issue, the bottom line was that for much of Pat's family, she was no longer really "one of them."

She was beginning to wrestle with this brutal reality when the baptism of a sixth grandchild (different family) occurred. This one was a nightmare of miscommunication right from the start. Pat heard that we were *both* invited, when in fact they intended for her to come alone. How these signals got crossed we will never know, but this was the family we weren't yet on good terms with so miscommunication was probably inevitable. I wanted to stay home and send Pat without me. *She* was the grandmother, *she* was the priest; I was the embodiment of "the problem." If not for me, they could all have continued their idyllic lives undisturbed.

"You *have* to go," Pat said to me. "They're doing the right thing by inviting us both, and we need to support that. Besides, I can't face it alone."

I agreed to go with her.

To keep the peace, to enable everyone to continue the fantasy that we really didn't exist as a couple, she volunteered to sit at the back of the church, far from the area reserved for the infant's family.

We arrived early that day, hoping to sneak in and be invisible. The priest, of course, was a colleague of Pat's, and was just walking down the aisle as we came in. I found a seat while he greeted her warmly, and then looked confused. "Won't you come to the altar with me to perform the ceremony?" he asked, clearly wondering why he had been asked to preside when the honor should have been hers. Pat explained briefly that co-celebrating with him would make things too awkward for everyone, and that she was happy just to be there. He took her by the arm and said, "Well, come up here and sit in the section reserved for the family!" She tried to protest that sitting in the back was fine, but he wouldn't hear of it.

I joined her in the last row of the family section after the priest had gone off to get ready for the service, and we waited, frozen with dread like prisoners awaiting execution. We had agreed not to be seen, and here we were sitting in plain view. "You're the grandmother," I kept reminding her. "You have a right to be here." She tried to get up to leave, but I held her leg down with my hand. "Staying here is the right thing to do. This is about the baby; you're here to witness the baptism."

The parents and siblings of the baby arrived and sat in the first row. They turned and saw us, and we smiled and waved, then saw their horrified looks. It would be over a year before we resolved the misunderstanding about my attending the ceremony; on that day, they thought our intention was to antagonize, to "shove our relationship in everyone's faces." *Why are you sitting here? You said you would sit in the back!* were the words that were hissed at her. Pat tried to mouth an explanation about the priest and the seating, but the congregation was arriving and they couldn't hear. We were devastated. How had it ever come to this? Pat's body was shaking and she tried again to get up and leave, but I held her in place. The church was filling up; to leave now would cause a scene. Besides, we saw the rest of the family arriving.

There are no words for the shock and disgust expressed in every aspect of their demeanor when they saw us. We felt like lepers. Hadn't they been told that we were coming? Didn't they know? Pat's ex-husband, her children and her grandchildren sat several rows in front of us. She sat behind her family, looking at their rigid backs, feeling their rejection, wanting to die. Not one of the adults acknowledged her presence. The grandchildren went back and forth between us and their parents, not sure what was going on but wanting to be loyal to both sides. We ached for them. If this was the worst day of my life, I couldn't imagine how it ranked in Pat's. Supporting her was all I could think to do, because it kept me from becoming violent. I sat up straight and pressed my shoulder against hers; I sang the hymns loudly; I attempted some kind of prayer, and was wracked with the irony of what was actually going on in the pews while we recited words about God's love and acceptance for all:

> Celebrant: Will you seek and serve Christ in all persons, loving your neighbor as yourself?
> People: I will, with God's help.
> Celebrant: Will you strive for justice and peace among all people, and respect the dignity of every human being?
> People: I will, with God's help.[1]

All eyes were on us as we walked to communion; our backs were on fire. I desperately wanted to take Pat's hand in mine, but lacked the courage. She was wearing her collar; they all knew who she was and the scandal she had caused. The words "grace under pressure" took on new meaning as I worked to breathe, to put one foot in front of the other, to kneel smoothly at the altar and not collapse, to sip and not choke on the wine.

And then, by the grace of God, it was over.

The church was still standing and the sky hadn't fallen, but for us it might as well have, as we watched her family slipping out the side door to avoid us.

The priest was in the aisle to greet people as they left. I'm not usually drawn to clergy (an odd admission under the circumstances), but when Pat introduced me and he shook my hand with a beautiful smile and said, *Welcome to our church*, I clung to his hand as if it were a life raft and I was drowning in the sea. My knees went weak and I couldn't let go of his hand; it was all I could do not to dissolve sobbing at his feet. *Thank you*, I finally whispered, *thank you*.

The rest of the day was a wash. We went home and tried to recover, but the pain was too deep to dislodge. We're both women, and we're both mothers. How many tears over the years have been dried on our breasts? We know how to hold one another, and so she lay in my arms with her head on my chest as her tears filled the room and the walls began to sway with the force of my anger.

How could they be so cruel?

The Red Door

. . . its true theme is a desire for the holy that, whatever form it takes, seems to be a part of the human condition . . .

Like the deer that yearns
for running stream,
so my soul is yearning
for you, My God . . .

—Kathleen Norris, *The Cloister Walk*

I grew up surrounded by old New England money in an eight bedroom house (mansion?) on the Elm-lined street sandwiched between the massive gothic buildings of what was then the Hartford Seminary and the formidable, arched structure of the Episcopal Diocesan House. Childhood afternoons were often spent "at play in the fields of the Lord" in tag football games on the Seminary grounds or roller-skating down the Diocesan House driveway. This subliminal, yet pervasive, ecumenical exposure during tender, impressionable years was complicated by the influence of my father, a man whose childhood wounding left him with a loathing of organized religion that knew no end. As irony would have it, he was the organist at the big Episcopal Church in town. "Catholics are the worst," my father always said on the subject of religion, "and Irish Catholics, the worst of the worst." Furthermore, he would say in lowered tones, "there's something 'funny' about the clergy—most of them seem to be gay."

My father's struggle with God led him, as our struggles often do, to get as close to religious ceremony as possible without actually having to participate. "I am a musician," he informed those in charge at the Episcopal Church when they hired him, "not a churchgoer." He maintained this stance, without wavering, for the duration of his employment. No one ever got my father to the altar. "Don't buy any of that religious crap," was the only spiritual guidance he gave his five children, who spent every Sunday in the church where their father played the organ and their mother sang in the choir.

This conflicted early religious experience fueled in me a lifelong fascination with churches and chapels, especially when they are empty and therefore completely still, and I have sought them in all my travels: The majestic stone-built, stained-glass-adorned temples that smell of the sacred and take my breath away, modern churches, ancient churches, wealthy churches, threadbare churches, Central American churches, ivy league college chapels, northern European churches, a lone church miles from any other structure at the bottom of a Scottish valley, a chapel in the Oregon woods facing a lake and a snow-capped volcano, the English church where King Henry VIII married Catherine Parr from whom my children are directly descended . . . I loved the Episcopal churches most because of the red doors, long before I knew that the red door was designed as a symbol of refuge and sanctuary for all who entered.

I am drawn to crosses. One of my mothers-in-law was a Presbyterian minister with expensive taste, exotic furniture, and a collection of crosses that might someday have been mine if I hadn't divorced her only son. When I think of all I gave up when that marriage fell apart, I think most of the crosses.

To this day, the sound of a pipe organ stops me awe-struck in my tracks and leaves me defenseless in its wake. Every cell of my body responds and if I listen long enough, my eyes close as tears stream down my face, and I see myself as a child turning in the pew to look up at the choir loft where, beneath the massive pipes in a long black robe, my father sat at the organ. I don't remember the prayers, the liturgy, the gospel readings, the creeds, or the sermons; I didn't understand religion at all and no one ever explained it to me. The closest I got to God in church was not at the altar; it happened on the special occasions when I was allowed to ascend the narrow stone steps to the choir loft and sit at the organ, bathed in stained-glass light, on the right side of my father. I remember the music. My God, the music! The hymns, the processionals and recessionals, the fugues, the trumpet voluntaries, the choir's tenors and sopranos, the swell of voices raised together in celebration, and the sight of my father at the organ, leaning into the pedals and keys and singing despite himself, a study of focus and passion, creating Heaven on earth with music *designed* to proclaim the glory of a God he could not name. Where did he think music comes from?

My father got as close to organized religion as he could by making the music. I did it by marrying the priest—a gay Episcopal priest who was raised Irish Roman Catholic.

Here I Am, Lord

Pat grew up on the fourth floor of an eleven-story high-rise apartment building in the "projects" on the lower east side of Manhattan, the daughter of a beautiful Lithuanian Jewish mother who loved people and laughter and dancing, and a bigoted, abusive, binge-drinking, Irish Catholic father whose only interests were money and social status. Her father was so embarrassed by his wife's Jewish heritage that he eventually convinced her to stop speaking the Yiddish she grew up with (and used to great advantage at the local Deli). With her long red hair and freckles, Pat's mother looked Irish, and that's the way Pat's father wanted it. Halfway through their marriage she converted to Catholicism.

Pat describes her mother as vibrant with life, compassionate, and very funny—with a brilliant gift for theatrics. "She looked like Lucille Ball. The two of us had the same sense of humor," she says. "We could make each other laugh so hard we'd be rolling on the floor and would have to crawl into separate rooms where we couldn't see each other in order to stop. That was the relationship I had with my mother." I never knew Pat's mother, but from the description I've always said that Pat's beauty and warmth must surely come from the Jewish side of her family.

Of her father she says simply, "He was the most selfish man I have ever known. He was a con artist. I was afraid of him."

Pat found happiness—and escape from household tension around her father's drinking and adultery—on the "project" playgrounds, where the kids from all the buildings met every free hour of the day. She was wiry, competitive, and fast; and she could outrun every boy her own age. These playgrounds nurtured the predominantly Irish Catholic high-rise children through formative years of inner city life. As an adult, Pat would write a children's book, *The Freckle Factory*, about those playgrounds and their impact upon her, for it was there—in what others might have called a world of cement—that she came to understand the power of community.

The Catholic Church, however, was the passion of Pat's life. The Church was where she learned about a loving Father, where she felt completely safe, where everything was sacred. By the time she was old enough to walk to school on her own, she was going to Mass every morning before classes—not because she was told to, but because she couldn't stay away. "I would talk to God," she says, "and I would hear God talking back. I knew at a very young age that God was actually in my heart, not in the church, but it felt like everything was *magic* in church—the bells ringing, the long steps I climbed to enter, the Latin which I knew by heart, and receiving communion—the 'body and blood of Christ.' If I could receive the body and blood of Christ every day, why wouldn't I want to do that? Church was where I felt holy, and good, and pure, and where the stains of my father's abuse could no longer touch me."

At school Pat's world was the Catholic nuns, whom she remembers as beautiful women. "So many people have had negative experiences in school with Catholic nuns, but I was very blessed," she says. "Our nuns really cared about us. They didn't go home to families at night, so they devoted their lives, and their love, to 'their' children. I know for sure that it was the nuns who kept many of the boys in my school off the streets, and I believe they shaped my life as well in many ways. I felt truly nurtured and loved by them, and sought their approval above all else, for through them, I could get closer to God."

Pat knew from early childhood that she was meant to be a priest. As a girl, she didn't know how that was going to happen, but her calling never wavered. When she got together with friends to play "make-believe," the others would be doctors, police, or teachers. She would dress up as a priest and set the table for communion. In church, she longed to be an altar boy! "I can't remember a time when I couldn't hear God's voice within me, or a time when I thought of doing anything else in the world but serving God," she says.

There would be mountains to climb before that happened, starting with the strain of a heterosexual marriage, which she entered at the age of 20, and the hell of five binge-drinking, drug-abusing years that began after the birth of her third child at the age of 24 and ended when she "bottomed out," was admitted to a rehab center and had a near-death experience. There were years of painful recovery and the marathon of going to school to finish her bachelor's degree and pursue a master's degree while raising young children in an era when most mothers stayed home. Eventually, Pat became a drug and alcohol counselor and hospice chaplain ("I learned to be a priest at Hospice," she says, "not in seminary."). Her heart-wrenching break with the Catholic Church preceded the long, tedious years of seminary at Yale Divinity School, which was so "heady" that for a time she completely lost a sense of God's presence in her life.

Finally, in her mid-forties, (on St. Bridget's Day) at a ceremony she never had fully believed was anything but an impossible dream, Pat put on a deep red robe and knelt before the bishop to say her vows. She was "examined" and found worthy. She was "vested" with the proper stole and given a bible. The bishop's hands were laid upon her. She was ordained an Episcopal priest. ". . .You are to love and serve the people among whom you work, caring alike for young and old, strong and weak, rich and poor . . . In all that you do, you are to nourish Christ's people from the riches of his grace, and strengthen them to glorify God in this life and in the life to come."[2]

So surreal for her was the reality of her ordination that she remembers only one detail of it—the music, and singing the hymn that had been in her heart for as long as she could remember:

Here I am, Lord.
Is it I, Lord?
I have heard You calling in the night.
I will go, Lord,
if You lead me.
I will hold Your people in my heart.[3]

The River

Imagine this. Imagine the Thames River in New London, Connecticut in the dead of winter at 5:30 in the morning. It's February of 1973, in fact; the first day of "spring training" for the Connecticut College women's crew team. The sun should be coming up any minute. We're out of shape after Christmas vacation, and we might just freeze to death. We find our oars and chip as much ice off them as possible before laying them in place on the dock. Then, we eight rowers and a coxswain enter the boathouse together, lift the long shell off its rack at the coxswain's command in one synchronized movement, and carry the lightweight form at shoulder height to the water. We stand at the edge of the dock, breathing together, waiting for the command to lower it into the river.

Starboard oars are put into the oarlocks with the handles lowered into the boat. Port oars go in next, then starboard rowers squat down, hold the dock, place their left feet gently into the boat against the wooden brace, and lower themselves onto their seats. One false move and any of us could put a foot through the shell's 16th-of-an inch-thick bottom. We sit, pull our right legs in, then hold the dock for port rowers to take their seats. No movement is wasted.

I'm not a morning person. The only reason I am on time for practice any morning of the season is because I sleep on the top bunk. The alarm clock is on the desk across the room and when it goes off, I throw myself off the bunk to stop the noise before it awakens my roommate. My crashing descent scares her cat out of a couple of lives, but she sleeps right through. In a daze, too tired to climb back to bed, I get dressed in as many layers as I can find in that state at that hour and join the rest of the team.

We push off from the dock and the rhythm begins to the coxswain's beat: *reach, dip, pull, release; reach, dip, pull, release*. We row without gloves to "feel" the oar, and to build calluses. Eight oars make their arcs in symbiotic movement with our hands and arms, *dipping, pulling, circling, dipping*. Eight rowers warm up: synchronize, *pull, breathe: extend, dip, pull, release*. Eight rowers create the set of the boat, gather speed, begin to soar. We're the elite. We're good. We're strong. We've got arms and legs of well-trained muscle that know what to do; we're competitive, and we can fly. One of us goes on to become an Olympic rower.

It's quiet on the river as the sun begins to rise. The water glistens. *Dip, breathe, dip, breath, dip, breathe - harder, longer, stroke, stroke, stroke, stroke* . . . We gasp for air, we bleed from blistered hands, our legs cramp and our arms seize up, but we work together like a well-oiled machine and we don't stop until we hear the command. And then we come down, slowly, slowly, slowly, slowly until we're gliding, "at the paddle"—*dip, breathe, dip, breathe, dip, breathe*. Eventually we are allowed to pull our oars into the boat with the handles in our laps, and we lie all the way back, legs outstretched, bodies at rest, water lapping at our sides, and knowing beyond all else that in that moment, we are the river and the river is us in the winter morning sun.

———

Years later I learn that all of us are made up of a "life-force energy" which flows through channels in our bodies like blood does through veins. When this life force energy becomes blocked through emotional, physical or spiritual distress, an imbalance is created which eventually produces physical symptoms. I'm hooked. I complete the master's degree I've begun, then immediately change fields to study the oriental healing arts. I become a shiatsu therapist. With hands, elbows, knees, and feet, light touch or deep pressure, I learn to work with points along the channels to release energetic blockages and stimulate the body's own healing power to eradicate symptoms. The Japanese call this a dance, for the "energy" of the practitioner and that of the client flow together in one synchronized movement.

Here, at last, was my calling—to a world of body-centered, spiritually-oriented work based upon the belief that within each person there exists an intrinsic drive toward wholeness, and the longing to unite with what mystics call the "Real Self."

The Real Self. Our life stories are written in the body, and the body never lies. The healing arts are about finding each person's "center:" the place called "home;" the place where truth lives. Miracles happen when you find the center. That which gives us life, which can't really be named, which goes way beyond a human ego so small that we constantly try to inflate it; that which flows and nourishes and heals, which has intelligence and memory, which nurtures every cell, every organ, every emotion and all of our spiritual potential, without which we don't exist—what happens to me when I work with *that* is what happens to Pat when she stands at the altar. Everything shifts, everything is different, in the presence of God.

"Touching" becomes my work in the world. I am the body person; I know who you are through your energy and the messages my body receives from relating to yours. Pat is the heart person; she knows who you are through compassion. When we meet, I teach her about the body, and she teaches me about the heart. At our spiritual best, like all human beings at their spiritual best, we can fly. For in that life-giving place that can't be named or fully understood, if we choose to row, *we are the river, and the river is us.*

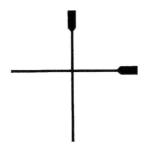

The Fence

The first time I married was for reasons that could have been featured in a pamphlet entitled: *If You're Getting Married For These Reasons, Don't*:

I was young and inexperienced.

I was raised by a mother who taught her daughters that a girl's purpose was to get married and have children, and a father who controlled the universe.

I had no sense of self-worth nor any confidence that I could handle the "outside world" on my own.

I went to a liberal arts college, studied Latin and French, and had no idea what to do with my life after that.

He fell in love with me.

He wanted to marry me.

He was tall, dark and handsome, impressed my parents, and would reflect well upon the family.

My younger brothers adored him.

He had a career with a guaranteed paycheck.

He knew how to control the universe.

It would be hard to describe the mess that occurred when my husband and I actually tried to have a relationship. Fortunately, this didn't come up very often. Most of the time he was away from home doing what it took to become the most highly-decorated young officer in the history of the Coast Guard. Our relationship wasn't tumultuous—it just wasn't loving or close. We coexisted for quite a while, yet I knew the moment our marriage ended, the moment every door in my fragile psyche slammed shut and it was over.

We were lying together in bed one evening, our 18-month old daughter asleep in the next room, and my husband informed me, so casually that it was almost in passing, that I wasn't "worth a shit" in bed.

The silence these words produced in me was so deep I believed I would never speak again, for society had taught me that the only way for women to earn their keep is to be pleasing to men. In particular, women need to be "good in bed." If I had failed at that, then there was, in fact, no reason for me to exist. It was another decade before I had the courage to leave that marriage, and I still didn't know I was gay. What I *did* know was that I had failed right to the core of heterosexual (and patriarchal) life.

———————

Twenty-two years later, this now ex-husband was one of the dignitaries hosting President George W. Bush at a ceremony for the president to "welcome the Coast Guard" into the newly formed Department of Homeland Security. The event was held safely inside a wrought-iron fence with heightened security by air and by sea. The "end" of the war with Iraq had just been declared (months, and probably years, prematurely), and there was a group of people led by an Episcopal priest friend of Pat's on the other side of the fence marching in protest of the president's military agenda and economic policies. My daughter was with her father as the troops marched "in review" on the parade grounds. Just beyond the marching, she could see the protestors out in the street, and among them, she said, was a woman walking along the wrought iron fence carrying a large rainbow flag with the word PEACE written in huge letters across the flag.

It was only to avoid embarrassing my daughter that I wasn't that woman carrying that flag, and I realized (with revelation's sting) that I hadn't failed, or been unworthy all those years ago; the problem had never been about my not "putting out enough" in the marriage, as my husband liked to explain it. The problem was that in every one of life's arenas, sexual orientation and otherwise, he and I were simply on opposite sides of the fence.

Leaving the Catholic Church

So many questions, I've never known anyone with so many questions, said Sister Mary V to Pat during their sessions of spiritual direction. It was within the years of recovery from her drinking and drug abuse that Pat had finally been able to feel again. What she had felt most in her daily meditations, for the first time in a long time, was the presence of God. She had begun to have mystical experiences that went far beyond her psychotherapist's ability to explain or understand, and had been referred to a cloistered Catholic nun who lived in the monastery one mile up the road from her house.

She would walk the mile to the monastery once a month to sit in a chair on one side of a half wall while Sister Mary V sat on the other side. Cloistered nuns are normally not allowed contact with the outside world, but the Mother Superior had heard about Pat's case and allowed them to meet.

"She was a holy presence," Pat said. "I could talk to her about God and she was the only person who ever understood the depth of the connection for me." They began each session with prayer. They said the rosary together and then talked about Pat's life. She told about hearing God speak to her and how it felt to enter into dialogue. She talked about seeing an incredible brightness around everything as if she were seeing the sun all the time, even in the rain. She tried to articulate how it felt to witness the "Christ" within her meet the "Christ" within others as she talked to them. Her mysticism was a gift, Sister Mary V assured her. She wasn't going crazy. The challenge was to integrate this gift into her daily experience.

They met this way for several years, and the relationship deepened. Pat began to mature. Her questions also went deeper and she began to chafe under the restrictions of the Catholic Church, especially as it related to women. Her calling, the burning desire to be a priest which she had carried since early childhood, had never gone away. One day she took a long walk up a very steep path in a nearby state park. The path took her to the top of a hill overlooking the Connecticut River Valley, and there she took her request to God: At the top of the hill she shouted her demand: "If you wanted me to be a priest, why did you have me raised in this religion? Tell me what to do!"

She waited.

Nothing happened.

So she started walking down the hill, and on the way down, it occurred to her with divine clarity that what she needed to do was to leave the Catholic Church!

"I need to realize my calling," she told Sister Mary V. "And in order to do that, I have to leave."

"You *can't* leave the Catholic Church," came the reply. If you do, then when you die you'll go straight to Hell."

"I just can't believe that," said Pat. *This is God's call to me.*

"If you do this, I can't see you any more," said Sister Mary V, "But I will pray for you."

They didn't meet again. This rejection was not her only loss. The Catholic Church had been Pat's lifeblood, its rituals the mainstay of her existence. Her family was Catholic. Her friends were Catholic. Her mentors were Catholic. When she left the Catholic Church, she left behind everything she had known of religious life.

With conflicted heart, therefore, she undertook the long, slow, grueling process of becoming an Episcopal priest. Eventually, she was ordained and assigned to a small, struggling parish. She had been serving there with great success for many years when she heard through a friend that Sister Mary V was dying and had been moved to a nursing home. Still a cloistered nun, she was not allowed to be seen, but Pat found out where she was and went to visit. Strangely, there was no one sitting vigil with Sister Mary V, as there should have been, when Pat entered the room. The elderly nun lay unconscious in bed, her hair, out of its habit, disheveled around her face. Pat knew that the beautiful nun would rather have died on the spot than be seen this way. She took a cloth and washed the nun's face; she brushed her hair and spoke to her gently. "I know you wouldn't want to be seen like this," she said as she brushed. "I want you to know how special you are to me, how much I have to thank you for, and how much I love you." She placed rosary beads into the nun's stiff hands and pressed the fingers closed. She began to recite the rosary as they had done together hundreds of times before. Sister Mary V's fingers began to move very slightly to find each bead; and as they prayed, a bright golden light appeared around the nun's body and hovered there. For quite a while Pat basked in that light. Then she finished her prayers, walked out of the room, and quietly closed the door.

> *Hail Mary, full of grace Our Lord is with thee. Blessed art thou among women and blessed is the fruit of thy womb, Jesus. Holy Mary, Mother of God, Pray for us sinners, Now, and at the hour of our death. Amen.*

If We Could Hold Hands Around the World

Think of the rays of the sun shining into houses. They are rays of the sun, and they are light, but they are attached to the sun and not to the houses. When the sun sets, their light no more remains.

What we have to do, then, is to become the Sun itself, so all fear of separation can forever be ended.

—Andrew Harvey, "Become the Sun Itself," in *Teachings of Rumi*

If we could hold hands around the world . . . I've heard Pat say so many times.

"Talk to me about faith," I then beg of her. "Tell me again about the 'Communion of Saints!'" I love the language she uses and the way the freckles in her eyes light up when she talks about God. "OK, here it is," she complies, and these are her words:

I believe that each of us is the light of the world—that each of us can erase pain and misery, because each of us can bestow the joy of angels.[4]

I believe that each of us can forgive our neighbor; and that every single one of us has the ability to remember our birth in the image of God.

I believe that when Christ's love is embodied in me, it will touch and call forth Christ's love within you. I believe that the core of each of us is the divine self, filled with God's light and able to work with the darkness that comes to meet us.

I believe that if we all held hands around the world we would form the living Christ. If we could do this, our dynamic human potential would be fulfilled. We would not only believe in the communion of saints, we would be the communion of saints joined as heavenly sisters and brothers. We would be able to forgive each other's sins. Imagine that . . . we would be able to forgive each other's sins.

The reality is that we can't form a circle of hands around the world. But if I can love God with all my heart and mind and soul, and love my neighbor as myself—as all the prophets and mystics have taught us to do—and if another can do the same, and another, and another . . . then the circle begins.

This isn't always easy. Most times, it doesn't even feel possible. When trouble arrives, when life is not peaceful, when prayer feels hollow and meaningless, when crisis prevails and trust is hard work, what then? That's when we need to pay attention, for faith is not anything that can be touched, or forced to happen, or even understood at times. Faith is what happens when one surrenders to God —when to feel separate from God's love would be like a stone at the bottom of a stream feeling separate from the water. Remember, as the mystic Rumi said, the wine of divine grace is limitless.

All faults come only from the faults of the cup . . .[5]

Coming Out

Freedom comes by staking a claim for one's reality in a world of 'majority rule.' It comes with those who risk the life they know for the life they dream can be.

—Marilyn Bennett Alexander and James Preston, *We Were Baptized Too*

At a point in every person's life, one has to look deeply into the mirror of one's soul and decide one's unique truth in the world, not as we may want to see it or hope to see it, but as it is.

—James E. McGreevey, Governor of New Jersey

Pat doesn't call it courage. She calls it the grace of God and *only* the grace of God, which enabled her, finally, to stop living a lie. For if you go deep within to find God, she says, "you eventually find yourself." She experienced the process deep within her body as a hand at the small of her back pushing her up and out, up and out. She resisted. She lay on the floor and banged her fists as she sent her cry to the Heavens: *What do I need to do?*

Are you willing to give up everything for me? was what she heard back.

She was. When Pat came out, she lost everything that constituted life as she knew it: her home and the town in which she had spent her adult life, her thirty-two-year marriage, her relationship with two of her three children and half of her grandchildren, and her church—the parish she had served with passion for many years. For a time, she lost her connection with God, for she could no longer hear God's voice within her heart. "I feel as though I've lost who I am," she would often say, because the person she had tried all her life to be was gone.

Coming out stories often include tales of suicidal depression, and Pat's story was no exception. There were moments when she talked about killing herself. There were entire days when we watched movies and ate chocolate so she wouldn't have to think or feel. There were times when she screamed and cried and smashed family photos and furniture out of sheer rage. And there were months on end when she would bury her head in her hands and say: *This is too hard. I can't do this—this is too hard. Maybe I should go back . . .*

The hardest thing about moving forward is not looking back. Life became a matter of deciding how to survive, one day at a time. She made appointments with her spiritual director. She received acupuncture treatments and Swedish massage, and she went to the chiropractor. She took homeopathic remedies for grief and depression. She talked to friends and supporters and looked up former mentors. We joined lesbian support groups and watched lesbian movies and overcame enough anxiety to go to lesbian dances (How were we supposed to dress? Did we look "lesbian enough?". . ."*too* lesbian?") We put a rainbow sticker on our car and practiced driving with it in public. She wrestled with her own strong homophobia and fear of being visible in the world as a lesbian woman, and as a lesbian priest. We went to meetings of the gay Episcopal group, Integrity. We spent a weekend first in Northampton, where she agreed to hold my hand in public only after she had seen five other lesbian couples holding hands (and then only under cover of darkness), and then in Provincetown, where you're expected to be gay and holding hands is the least of what people do on the streets.

The news spread in the town where Pat had spent so many years. Leaving one's husband for another woman in a small town is big news. It was not a friendly divorce. To her utter amazement (since she wrestled with the all-encompassing homophobia that was shared, she assumed, by everyone she knew), people sought her out to offer support. She received cards and phone calls from people she hadn't seen in ten or twenty years; others greeted her in public by saying, "You may not remember me, but I've heard your story, and I want to say how much I admire your courage." She drew great strength from this support, and from the support of many others who surprised her with their unconditional love, such as my 15-year-old daughter who, when asked if she would be embarrassed to bring her friends home to a gay mother and her partner said, "If my friends aren't mature enough to deal with it, then they're not mature enough to be my friends!" And the conservative couple across the street who said, "Tell Pat to come out of hiding; we're very accepting here!" And her grandson's nursery school teacher who sought her out to say, "I've heard about you because my friends go to your church; I just want you to know how much I admire who you are." And a young woman who used us as role models because she, too, was struggling to come out. And my 18-year-old daughter who brought home *two* potted plants for Mother's Day and said, "We've never seen our mother so happy." And even a new neighbor who said, when we cautiously mentioned our homosexuality, "Oh I know! It's fine with me—I've told everyone on the street!" (Be careful what you wish for.)

Slowly, as she came out of crisis, Pat began to claim her sexuality as a gift. She began to understand that coming out of hiding for homosexuals is a sacred journey, and she began to feel a sense of responsibility to others struggling with the issues she had resolved to come to terms with, especially within the Church. When this happened, her desire to live—and her passion for ministry—returned. She began to speak in public and became active in the gay civil rights movement; she encouraged her bishop to become proactive in support of gay rights within the Episcopal Diocese; she told her story wherever it was needed to offer support and encouragement; she talked with legislators in support of "gay marriage," and she answered questions for anyone who asked them. Gay people in crisis were referred to her in an unending stream, and she agreed to see them at any time day or night. Eventually, as Pat began to move in the world as the person she *is* rather than the person others *want* her to be, she began to heal. And finally, she could allow herself to feel the joy, the delayed "coming home" of the soul that makes the whole world feel "like a black-and-white movie that has suddenly converted to color."[6] Before too long, we moved to the forty acres of land that had been given to Pat with the sole stipulation that she use it "for the glory of God"—a lifetime removed from that fateful day when she raged and railed against the crushing admission that she was homosexual.

The Truth

I state right from the outset: 'Be not afraid!' This is the same exhortation that resounded at the beginning of my ministry in the See of Saint Peter . . . Of what should we not be afraid? We should not fear the truth about ourselves.

—Pope John Paul II

Writing about Pat's marriage to her husband was the most difficult part of this book. Usually, in collecting the words for her part of the story, I would talk with her for as long as it took until I was confident that the material was honestly, nakedly reflecting her experience. When it came to her marriage, however, nothing worked. We talked. She cried. I took excerpts from her journal entries and letters with her permission and tried to piece them together, but they didn't reflect the whole. How could I possibly put into narrative the intimacy of a marriage between Pat and the man she had loved as a brother for thirty-two years? How to describe with any reliability the pain of trying to work the unworkable? How possibly to describe the agony and the loss when, finally, she had no choice but to look into his eyes and say she was leaving?

Pat and her husband met as teenagers at a college dance in New York City and in those days they had everything in common: they loved sports, dancing. They both came from conservative Irish Catholic families (in his parents' case, directly from Ireland), and they both wanted children. Above all, they could make each other laugh. They married young and became the model heterosexual couple.

They had every intention of growing old together. Not until Pat became conscious enough to examine the story of her life did she admit what they had both "known" at some level for three decades: that the insurmountable problem in their marriage (which divided them even as their love was uniting them), "from the wedding night through to the day she left," she wrote, "was, and always would have been, my homosexuality." Her husband spent the years of their marriage trying to achieve the impossible—physical and emotional intimacy with a wife whose natural way is to find physical and emotional intimacy with a woman. The awkwardness of the honeymoon was mitigated when the bed frame broke and they landed on the floor to laugh long and hard, but the theme of failed sexual intimacy grew and festered, and finally became a sore too raw even to talk about. Pat remembers throwing a radio through the second story window in raging frustration as she felt her husband's anger year after year and increasing loss of interest. She struggled with constant feelings of inadequacy, isolation, abandonment, and the shame that seems to be written into homosexual DNA. The unwritten contract they had was that she carry the burden for their marital problems alone. "Taking on single responsibility for our lack of physical intimacy, and the toll that took on our marriage, left me feeling as though I was leading a double life," she wrote in a letter after she left her husband. "I didn't tell you what was going on inside of me because I accepted your diagnosis that the 'problem' was mine to 'fix.' This is where our lack of communication began and ended. You didn't know me, and couldn't, because in those days I didn't even know myself."

Their marriage didn't work, and it wasn't for lack of trying. The closest they came to admission, however, was to simply turn off the TV when anything on the subject of homosexuality was being shown, for that was the undercurrent in their relationship they wouldn't go near. In the early years she drank alcohol, took "speed" and hung out with other young wives who did the same. She played softball all summer and spent every spare moment with her friends from the team, many of whom she ran into again years later after they, too, had come out. She went to doctors to ask why sex was so painful ("you're athletic and your muscles are tight," they said, "just try to relax," which was about as helpful as the "just close your eyes and think of England" advice Victorian mothers once gave their daughters). She made close women friends, about whom her husband bitterly complained, and brought them home to become "part of the family." They were her surrogate partners everywhere but in the bedroom, and in one case (during the drinking years) even there. At one point, she thought about leaving the marriage but in those days, that choice was too terrifying to make. What framework or support would a good Irish Catholic girl living in the isolation of a "closed" family and religious system have had for "coming out" and getting divorced? Lesbianism and divorce are right up there with birth-control and abortion as tickets straight to Catholic Hell.

A problem that is never addressed eventually poisons the family system and Pat's family is a textbook example. "Think of all that could have been avoided if I had felt empowered to claim my sexuality in my late twenties when I first became aware of it," she wrote, in a letter she never sent, about that early period in their lives. "The years of my substance abuse, the "Daddy's a saint, Mommy's a problem/good-parent, bad-parent dynamic which evolved very subtly as frustration grew and which still forms the core of the family belief system, our daughter's long-standing verbal attacks as she absorbed the unnamed marital anger and directed it towards me, and my constant pulling away from home, which left my children feeling that I had abandoned them. To this day, most of the family have never healed."

Eventually Pat cleaned up her act, got into recovery, tried to have an honest, open relationship with her husband, and went to seminary. Even then she suffered from blinding headaches which left her incapacitated and became another way to avoid the marital bed, and even then, her closest connection was with women. The issue never went away because it had never been resolved. "How tragic," she wrote, "to think of the effort it took for us to present as the perfect household while this chaos was raging underneath. Most of the time, in fact, I could hardly breathe with the effort. Imagine how different our lives could have been, and how much healthier we all would now be, if we had simply accepted the truth."

The truth, which took fifty-two long years for Pat to claim and which the man she still loves won't discuss with her even now, was the only "fix" for the problem.

Brotherly Love

Once we begin to see each other as the 'culmination of a billion-year process' and realize that we are not different or separate but actually made of the same stuff as the stars, we will learn to truly honor each other—and racism, sexism, homophobia, and other social and economic inequities will naturally fall by the wayside.

—Christian de la Huerta, *Coming Out Spiritually*

Dear Pat,

". . . It is obvious you need help (*I say this with love*) . . .The decision you made to 'come out' was and is wrong. You should have suppressed your feelings and prayed with all your might to your God to help you either find a way to live a 'straight' life style, or the strength to suppress it so as not to bring the hurt and stress on your family.

If need be, you should have taken your secret to your grave rather than come out . . . as a priest, how can you sin against God as you have? You know what the Bible says about homosexuality. Is what you've done more important than the vows you made as a wife and a priest? *Why has your faith been so weakened?*

As religion teaches, there is good, and there is evil. You've fallen from grace and are in a world where evil is. You need to come back.

. . . Do not become a champion for the gay life style. Do not preach in favor of the life style. Gays do themselves harm when they constantly throw it in the faces of people. There are many more important issues in this world than the furtherance of a life style which is not considered the norm and never will be . . .

You need to go to your family and ask for their help. You need to say you're sorry to your family.

You need to fight to recover the things that are much more important than a life style that is a sin—your children, your grandchildren, your husband.

You must demand that God take you back in His arms and love you again. We all still love you and always will, but we want to come first. That's the way it is. That's the way of things. Learn to like yourself, but your family is first, always first.

I hope you can get out of the evil world . . . there is help waiting. I'll always love you as my sister. As a person, what you've done is wrong and a sin against God. Stop what you're doing and come back to the good world—it is very nice here—God is here. Jesus is waiting for you. He forgives you. He told me so."
Love, D

No One Will Take Your Parish Away

Most tribes, particularly before the relentless and often violent impact of Christianity, considered (gay people) special, and honored them as recipients of special powers because they were in between the sexes, and could therefore perceive and understand both realities.

—de la Huerta, *Coming Out Spiritually*

The Church in all its glory has convinced us that to express a major part of our created selves would be a terrible sin . . . Silencing destroys dreams and provides fertile ground for resentment about the church, about God, and even about self.

—Marilyn Bennett Alexander and James Presson, *We Were Baptized Too*

Will I lose my parish? she asked the Bishop.

It was the end of summer, and the church calendar was about to resume its active life with the autumn migration towards Advent and the Christmas season. Pat and I had known each other for seven months. Three months had come and gone since she had left her husband. It was time to address all of this with the Episcopal Diocese.

Coming out to the Diocese was, for Pat, one of those occasions where beforehand you don't know how you'll get through it, and afterwards don't know how you did. But she was met with gentleness and understanding. *No one will take your parish away from you,* said the Bishop. She could breathe again. Life might go on, she thought.

At some point between that day in September and the

end of November two months later, there was a change of heart within the system. Perhaps it came with the onset of Thanksgiving where, upon reflection, no one in church authority was feeling particularly thankful for a priest who chose to "come out of the closet" within months of the Bishop's date of retirement. What Bishop in his right mind would want to leave office under a hail of controversy?

On Thanksgiving *night*—giving us all time to eat a large meal and settle into complacency by the hearth in front of the fire—the phone rang. It was the assistant Bishop, calling Pat with the news that she was, in fact, going to lose her job and her church. Why he couldn't manage, in all his wisdom and pastoral expertise, to break this news to her on a day—any day—other than the one created for giving thanks, remains a mystery.

Homosexuality was never mentioned as the reason for the Bishop's decision; he used a technicality of Canonical law regarding divorce as grounds for dismissal and fooled no one. Pat's congregation was furious. The people raged. They called the Diocese in protest. They stood up in church when the Bishop arrived to give them the news and said, "We're angry and our anger is not going to go away . . . she's our priest, and *we don't care if she's gay* . . . she's taught us about unconditional love; why won't you let us give her unconditional love?" To no avail.

The Bishop was a black man. You'd have thought he would have understood oppression. He pointed out that the Bible condemns homosexuality; she pointed out that the Bible condones slavery. They had been friends. The last meeting between them was surreal, she said, because the Bishop did the unthinkable—he knelt and kissed her hand.

"I'm sorry," he said, "but I have to do what I have to do."

"And I have to do what I have to do," she replied, begging him to rise.

Then she walked out of the door and into the void.

Falling in Love

Lovers don't finally meet somewhere. They're in each other all along.

— Rumi

She's the love of my life, my daughter remembers me saying.
WHY is she the love of your life? She asked.
Well look at it this way, I apparently said, *she's left-handed and I'm right-handed,*
so when we share a coffee mug across a table
we can each reach for it without shifting the mug.

One August morning I went to see a psychic in Worcester, Massachusetts who was highly recommended. She put me on a massage table in a darkened room full of soft purple strobe lights and the chant of the "eternal OM" coming from wall speakers. Purple, she explained, is very powerful for discouraging "negative entities." This woman used a "scanning" method to do her readings: running her hand down the outside of the left leg gave her past life information, and running her hand down the right side gave her information about the future—up to about two years into the future, she said.

I told her a bit about my life, and asked for information about my next partner, for I knew that the next person with whom I fell in love would be a woman. It seemed I could *feel* her already; my heart would leap with joy at unexpected moments and the sensation seemed undeniably tied to the female partner I had yet to meet.

The psychic did the past life reading first, and told me I had been royalty (probably many times) that I had been hung or choked to death for abusing my power, and that I had been betrayed by the people I trusted. Fine. I had been told all this before.

Then she began to read the future by scanning my right leg. Without hesitation, she described the partner who, she said, was definitely a woman. This woman, she said, was some kind of healer or in some kind of ministry, was shorter than I and plumper, and had sparkly eyes. She said that I would be moving to a new house and this woman would join me there. She saw us as very happy together. Then her faced turned red and she said "Oh, my!"

"What are you seeing?" I asked.

"Making love," she said. "Lots of making love . . ."

"What does it look like?" I asked naively.

"Very nice . . . oh yes, it's very nice," she mumbled, and brought the session to a close before I could press her for the details.

"When will this woman and I get together?" I asked

"Eighteen months," she said.

———————

Since I had no plans to move from the rental house into which I had fled after my second divorce, and since I knew no woman of the psychic's description, the entire reading seemed like a waste of time and money.

Before we met, Pat and I had a mutual friend who told each of us she would introduce us to the other, but somehow never got around to it. As soon as I heard Pat's name, I was interested. As soon as she heard my name, she was interested. We didn't meet for months, and then we met by chance in our friend's driveway as Pat was leaving and I was arriving.

I remember every detail of what I wore and how I looked—the comfortable black pants and favorite blue sweater that exactly matched my eyes, the lace-up boots from a trip to London, and the fact that, for once, I liked the way my hair had decided to arrange itself that afternoon. I remembered all this because for days afterwards I wondered if she liked what she saw. I came bouncing out of the car to say hello and we were introduced. "So you're Pat," I said. "And you're Karen!" We shook hands and she placed her second hand on top of mine the way she does when greeting people and I heard my heart whisper, *There she is.*

A week later, we met again with our friend to talk about the healing center she was hoping to build. My job was to bring lunch. The best sandwich in town was the chicken and sliced grape salad sandwich from the local deli, and nothing else would do but to replicate it with my own hands. This was odd in itself since I don't like to cook. It took two days. I bought the highest-quality roasting chicken, carefully removed the skin, cooked it, let it cool overnight, and took all the meat off the bone. I bought the very best bread. I looked long and hard for grapes that were sweet, for it was December and grapes were not in season, and I carefully sliced them. No sandwich was ever more lovingly assembled and wrapped, no presentation more flooded with significance than the moment I handed Pat her lunch and said, "I made this for you."

Our love felt ageless, centuries old. From the touch of

our hands in greeting, we recognized one another. From our first interactions, a deep and intimate love for one another was undeniable. Who knows how many lifetimes we've been together before, but until the words "I'm gay, and I've known it all my life" came out of Pat's mouth six months later and changed her footing forever, there was no way to be together in this one. Somewhere in the depths of those words she found the strength to leave a thirty-two year marriage and a life that was always predictable and completely secure—a life in which nothing ever changed. She, who had already raised her children and had for years avoided living with pets, left everything that was familiar to her and came to live with me, my two adolescent children, a large German Shepherd, and three long-haired white cats in my new house, eighteen months to the day from my visit to Worcester, Massachusetts.

The Bread of Heaven, the Cup of Salvation

There is no one brought up in the Judeo-Christian tradition who does not have to come to terms with the life and teachings of Jesus. This is true for Christians and Jews alike. It is also true for atheists or agnostics. Jews need to understand and accept the transmission of faith Jesus brought to them. Christians need to understand how his teachings of love and forgiveness have been inverted into teachings of fear and guilt. Atheists need to understand his revolutionary message of equality.

—Paul Ferrini, *Love Without Conditions*

A nightmare at the age of six caused me to wake up screaming and my mother to come running. In the dream I walked through our kitchen to the door of the basement stairs and stood looking down the steep steps into the dark. I knew I had to go down, but I hung back, dreading the descent. Finally, I went slowly down the steps and peered around the corner. There I saw God lying on the floor without a head. That's when the screaming started.

I was so shaken by the nightmare that my mother could hardly convince me to tell her about it. Eventually the words came, and she listened quietly before asking, "What did God look like? "You can't see God," I explained to her, "but I knew it was Him. He was lying there on the basement floor, and he had no head."

What is astounding about this nightmare is that "God" was never discussed in our household. Religion, if mentioned at all, was sneered at and dismissed ("the virgin birth and the resurrection are stories so preposterous," my father said, "that only the faithful could accept them.") My nightmare occurred before I was ever taken to church, which happened when I was ten. At the age of six, no adult had ever talked with me about God.

The psychological implications of my dream are probably endless. Basements, like tunnels, often symbolize the unconscious. The beheaded form could have represented the fact that I had reached the age when most children in our culture lose (repress) their inherent, "felt" sense of God because it isn't nurtured or named; it "dies" therefore and becomes buried in the unconscious. In religious families the child's natural, embodied connection with God is replaced by the imposition of an "outer" God, which is described and defined by the Church.

The dream could also have represented the separation of head (brain) from body (heart/compassion/love) that is rampant in our society—both in church and everywhere else. Or, it could have been about the fact that when I was six years old, my mother gave birth to her first son after having three daughters. Living in a family that wanted boys, I remember the feeling that nothing about me would ever be as important to my parents as that event. I was the first child, but *he* was the first *son*; any chance of having the (unconditional, "divine") love I craved ended with his birth because I would never be a boy.

———————

There is no denying that the Christian heritage is a part of who I am at a cellular level, despite having grown up with no real knowledge or understanding of it. I have always been gripped with an unrealized longing to "connect." We all have this. Every one of us, they say, is seeking God whether we know it or not. This longing progressed from my fascination with churches and crosses to a conscious ache once I met Pat. I asked a lot of questions. She tried to explain the trappings of her religion to me and I tried to pay attention. I desperately wanted to find a place larger than I was to feel "at home." The world and verbiage of the church, however, took some getting used to. I didn't know, for example, that all bishops wear purple shirts. The first time I saw one, I thought the bishop was supporting gay rights and complimented him on the choice of color. I laughed when I heard Pat refer to the "Daily Office," because her New York accent turned it into "daily orfice," which I heard as daily *orifice* and couldn't figure out why anyone would use it as a basis for prayer, whatever it was. Was the Bishop's "Deployment Officer" to be saluted? Did the "Canon to the Ordinary" fire off metal balls at non-church-goers and what, pray tell, was "the Ordinary?" Could Junior and Senior "Wardens" be anything other than prison guards or "Primates" other than monkeys? "Custody of the eyes," brought to mind a slogan for eye make-up, and the "Court of Arches," sounded for all the world like a rose garden. Furthermore, it was only in reference to the Bloody Mary's my parents drank after church on Sundays that I ever heard the term "a thirst after righteousness!"

Then there was religious content to grapple with. I just couldn't accept that people actually *believe* the Bible to be "the word of God," and Jesus to be, literally, *the* "son of God." Don't they know that we are *all* children of God and that the story of Jesus is a myth, which has ageless lessons to teach *only* if taken symbolically? To take the archaic, fairly incomprehensible Sunday morning readings literally—no matter how beautifully written—seemed beyond belief, for they were written in another age, in another language, for people with whom we have no current cultural or perceptual common ground and then altered significantly in repeated translations. I couldn't comprehend the appeal of a system as rigid, inflexible, and unchanging as the creed, doctrine, and dogma of the church. Christianity has taught since the Middle Ages that "the Church is indivisible, the afterlife a certainty and all (religious) knowledge is already known. And nothing will ever change."[7] How could this be taken as a reflection, even in small part, of the mystery and expansiveness of God-given life with all its movement, variety, growth, and *constant* change? I tried to quiet my doubts, however. As unschooled as I was in the ways and teachings of religion, who was I to question two thousand years of Christian establishment? Then I happened upon Stephen Mitchell's book *Jesus, What He Really Said and Did*, which was written after a study of the Gospels in their original Greek, and my religious education began:

> *The composition of the Gospels is a very complex subject, but in brief here is what I discovered. Jesus never wrote anything himself. The earliest account we have of him is the Gospel According to Mark, which dates from around the year 70, forty years after Jesus' death.*
>
> *The Gospels of Matthew and Luke probably date from the decade between 80 and 90, and the Gospel of John probably from between 90 and 100. None of these books*

was written by a direct disciple of Jesus. Jesus did have disciples named Matthew and John, but they weren't the authors of the Gospels attributed to them. The Gospels were written in Greek, a language Jesus may or may not have known. His language was Aramaic, which is a cousin of Hebrew. His original words, in the original Aramaic, may never have been written down; if they were, they have been lost (except for one word, abba, which means 'father'). Some of the stories and reports were handed down orally from Jesus' own disciples, who lived with him and knew him, even if they didn't always understand his teachings.[8]

And so on.

I started reading the works of Bishop John Shelby Spong (the most "radical bishop in the world," according to some), and I saw that he, after a lifetime within the church and I, the consummate "un-churched" (as if "church" could be either a verb or an adjective) neophyte, had come to the same conclusions:

The words of the Apostles' Creed, and its later expansion known as the Nicene Creed, were fashioned inside a worldview that no longer exists . . . The way reality was perceived when the Christian creeds were formulated has been obliterated by the expansion of knowledge. That fact is so obvious that it hardly needs to be spoken . . . Institutional Christianity seems fearful of inquiry, fearful of freedom, fearful of knowledge—indeed, fearful of anything except its own repetitious propaganda, which has its origins in a world that none of us any longer inhabits.[9]

In *Here I Stand*, Spong writes:

It . . . made me begin to realize that all the barriers we institutional people had placed into the life of the church as a way of keeping pure and exclusive our claims to be the sole agents of God on this earth were now inoperable. The idea that the only channels God would use to reach people with grace were the institutionalized Christian sacraments was itself strange. The claim that these sacraments could be celebrated and administered only by those who had been officially ordained and thus empowered by the church to accomplish the opening of these channels of grace suggests that God somehow works for the church or that the church somehow controls God . . .

I also began to look at the creeds in a new way. An elementary study of the formation of the creeds in the third, fourth, and fifth centuries will reveal that the process that produced them was deeply political and highly compromised. The creeds were more about power than they were about truth. That some came to be called 'orthodox' and their version of Christianity designated 'orthodoxy' was not necessarily a recognition of who was right, but a recognition of who had won. A primary purpose of the creeds was not to spell out the Christian faith, but to exclude competing groups and their competing versions of truth from the church's life.[10]

"If you believe that every word in the Bible is dictated by God," says author Richard Holloway in his book, *Doubts and Loves, What is Left of Christianity*, "then you are going to have massive problems with contemporary society, particularly with the liberation of women."[11]

"Most of today's religions (in fact) are concentration camps of the patriarchy," says mystic Andrew Harvey.[12]

―――――――――

I read Marcus Borg's books *Meeting Jesus Again for the First Time*, and *The Heart of Christianity*, John Shelby Spong's books *Why Christianity Must Change or Die*, *Here I Stand*, and *Born of a Woman*, and Richard Holloway's book *Love and Doubts*, *What is Left of Christianity*, and felt a profound sense of relief to find that there are theologians, scholars, and other courageous, highly intelligent, and compellingly-articulate renegades who understand that neither the mystery of life nor the teachings of Jesus have anything to do with the man-made, fear-and-control-based trappings of the organized religion we've come to know for thousands of years. There *are*, it turns out, modern day prophets and many others who are leaving what Marcus Borg calls the "earlier paradigm" of Christianity which sees Christianity as grounded in divine authority and the Bible as a *divine product*, and are moving steadily into an *emerging paradigm*, which sees the Bible metaphorically and Christian life as a life of *relationship and transformation*.[13] Confident that my religious heritage was in good hands, I could stop my questioning along those lines.

What I continued to wonder was whether there was anything that religion, as it had been molded by the Church, *did* have to offer me to still the longing—was there anything at all to hold on to?

Here's what I discovered in the exploration, and what I believe to be true: No bastardization over the millennia has been able to stamp out the fact that somewhere deeply embedded in "organized" Christianity is what Bishop Spong calls "Christpower." Some people call it the *Christ mind*. Somewhere buried in the Christian church are remnants of what we know about the *real* life and death of Jesus Christ and the real message he (and many others) brought to the world, a message based upon "the sense of love, forgiveness, expanded life, and expanded being . . ."[14] Or, as Richard Holloway puts it, "No one *has* to follow the Christian path . . . But you might just fall into it from sheer joy at its possibilities."[15]

In its *pure form*, there is something mystical about the church, about the priesthood, and about the teachings of Jesus Christ. This mysticism calls to me like a Siren. Watching Pat at the altar, seeing and feeling the ritual, the consecration of the elements, and the reverence of the cross, my whole being, inexplicably, goes still. Spell-bound, I hear her begin:

> *Almighty God, to you all hearts are open, all desires known, and from you no secrets are hid.*
> *Cleanse the thoughts of our hearts by the inspiration of your holy spirit, that we may perfectly love you, and worthily magnify your holy name . . .* [16]

There is something riveting and indefinable within these words, this ritual—something mysterious, something bigger than I am. Something that could hold me in its embrace or that I could hold within mine. There is something, like the silence of the ocean floor, that is "ancient."[17]

———

Of course I was never baptized, which kept me barred (excuse the pun) from the communion rail the few times I attended church as an adult for weddings or baptisms or accompanying friends. Just as well, I thought—how would I know what to do? In the early stages of our relationship, when Pat and I were "just" friends, she performed a baptism to which I was invited. I explained that I was not a legitimized Christian and therefore couldn't take communion. "Today is an ecumenical service," she said. "I'll give you communion."

The Holy Eucharist held no significance for me except as a source of worry about how to receive the host, when to dip or sip, and how not to make a fool of myself in front of the priest with whom I happened to be in love.

I held out my hands as I saw the others do and received "the body of Christ, the bread of Heaven." Then came the cup and I took it to my lips: "The blood of Christ, the cup of salvation." My heart began to pound, and my body began to shake—obviously a reaction to my feelings for her, I thought. I sat alone in the pew for a long time after the service. Everyone was at coffee hour and no one missed me. The shaking didn't stop. What was it? I looked at the cross that hung up high at the front of the church, and something about it held my gaze. As I continued to look, there came a tearing in my chest as if my heart was breaking open, and there it was—*there was the connection*, coming to me in a way I could never have anticipated, for suddenly I saw; suddenly I knew—not because I had heard the words, but because I could feel the dying of Christ. I felt the crucifixion: the yearning he had to reach us, the pain he bore, the purity of his love, the burning in his eyes, the gentle, gentle heart and tortured body, the desperate knowing that most of us would never understand, the way he saw hundreds of years into the future and knew that he hadn't accomplished enough. This is what I knew without knowing how I knew it. I was looking at a cross that had no figure on it, and yet he looked at me, and I couldn't forget his eyes.

"At this moment," I wrote of this mystical experience, "I can feel the joy in his chest; he's still on that cross, but I see him lower his head as tears fall, in acknowledgment that (finally, finally) I am beginning to understand. He's weary and his arms ache, but he won't move until every single one of us understands and can feel the love he holds, the agony he carries, the pain and ecstasy of surrender. He knows, in fact, that he'll be on that cross forever. I would give anything to wash his feet or hold his aching body—to ease his pain even for a moment. But the only way to ease his pain is to move in the world with his love in my soul, and to let my eyes burn with the passion in his heart."

I have never been able to achieve this, even in part, but I realize now that *this* is what the church has been trying to teach for over 2,000 years. No wonder the mystics went mad—how could anyone have thought this could be put into words?

Filial Love

Homosexuality is an abomination . . . it says so in the Bible. I don't want to get involved.

This was the response of Pat's youngest son to the news that his mother is gay. Well into adulthood when he had this reaction, he is a person who neither reads the Bible nor attends church, yet he said these words, walked out of his mother's life, and to our knowledge has never looked back.

He is the child who was in high school when his mother finally made her break with the Catholic Church and became an Episcopal priest. He wrote a school assignment about that pivotal transition (emphases mine), and I quote:

My life has been full of positive influences and strong role models. One of the most inspiring people in my life has been my mother. *She has overcome obstacles and made her way into a profession once reserved for men only. As long as I can remember, my mother has been a person with a calling. Her calling was to the priesthood, but as a married, female Catholic, this seemed impossible . . .*

. . . Being a devoted Catholic with a strong background in Catholic school made her decision an even harder one. She couldn't ignore what her soul knew was right. *Thus, she decided to leave her Church and join the Episcopal religion. Getting into the process to qualify for the priesthood was no easy task. This meant going back to school, yet again. It also entailed a very grueling, intense schedule between school, work, and home—not to mention being under the constant scru-*

tiny of the board evaluating her every move. Thinking back, she really managed the impossible. *This past summer my Mom reached her first goal of being ordained a deacon, and this coming month, I will participate in the service when my Mom is ordained a priest.*

I learned a lot from this experience. I used to take her for granted and assumed she did what all moms do. But, she is extremely unique. Not only has she reached her dream, *but she has gone further than women are 'supposed' to go. She overcame all barriers in her way and came out victorious. Sure, there were many nights when she was unsure and scared, but with support and love she has become an inspiration to everyone who is blessed with knowing her.*

———————

Had this boy *not* been raised within the Roman Catholic Church, which represses human sexuality in all its forms, and within a family whose operating strategy was to deny the homosexuality in its midst, he might well have been able to write a very similar and equally loving piece about his mother's coming out. Instead, he made his rigid pronouncement, went on with his life, got married, had children, and never initiated contact again.

This is the abomination.

Contrasts

. . . Homosexuality and the issue of same-sex marriages is inherently a moral and religious matter. . . Those with a proclivity to homosexuality are no different than those predisposed to heterosexual philandering, alcoholism, drugs, or gambling. They're slaves to sin and Christ offers hope to those under this yoke. The church must have its doors wide open for those seeking refuge, hope, and freedom from sin, read the editorial in a local paper on July 5th, 2003.

—Ray Jones, Jr., Baptist Minister

Y ou will always be welcome with us," my older daughter wrote to Pat the same year. "I'm sorry about some of your children. There is no excuse to be so hurtful. Their actions are selfish, and it is sad to think that they live by such rigid rules and are so inflexible that they would rather reject you than accept a new relationship with their mother," she wrote. "Your children are not setting a good example for their children, or for my sister and me, who are living the other half of exactly the same situation. Someday they will grow up and realize that life is too short to live it in anger; that acceptance of those you love is a valuable gift. But by then it will be too late. They will have wasted years they could have spent with you. You won't lose your grandchildren, because all kids want to spend time with their grandmothers! And not to worry, if I ever have children, you will always be invited. . ."

*As a pastor, I believe homosexuality and same-sex mar-
riages are immoral and therefore detrimental to society . .
. we are on a slippery slope. Homosexuals have histori-
cally been inclined to post pubescent boys who have not
yet reached manhood.*[18]

"I am honored to have Pat as part of my family," my
younger daughter wrote to us during a particularly difficult time in the transition. "It seems like such a shame that
I am able to enjoy Pat's company, friendship and mother-
ing more than some of her own kids can . . . I have wanted
nothing more than happiness for you, mama, and I don't
think there has ever been a time in my life when I remember you laughing so much and crying so little! In these last
years, due to the fact that you seem more comfortable with
who you are . . . our relationship has done nothing but im-
prove. I would support you with whomever you may
choose: now having said that, I am glad that you and Pat
have chosen one another because she is an awesome person. I give nothing but thanks for the time when she came
into our lives . . . I wish that could ease some of her pain."

*I will continue to treat them (homosexuals) as children of
God, sinners like the rest of us who need God's grace and
forgiveness. I will also continue to pray that they see the
errors of their way and repent.*

—Statement by an Episcopal priest in McCook, Nebraska, who entered
Seminary after retiring from 23 years of service in the U.S. Marine
Corps.[19]

Reunion

Pat "came out" and divorced within a family that doesn't address conflict or change, a family where no matter how many dead elephants are lying in the middle of the room, the elephant issue is never discussed.

"I'm gay, and I need to leave this marriage," was probably the most honest statement made in that setting in thirty years, and it resulted in a level of shock, anger and upheaval so violent that communication between Pat and most of her family came to a stand-still for many long months. Time passed however, as it always does, and emotions eventually softened or wore themselves down enough that we took the risk of planning a luncheon. This created an onslaught of uncertainties and points of anxiety for us (and I'm sure for them, although true to form, these matters were not discussed), the most basic being: Would the two and a half-year-old even remember her "Nana," much less know what to make of me? How do you explain homosexuality to a two-year-old?

It was because of me (they said) that the children's parents hadn't allowed the children to visit for over a year; they didn't "know" me well enough, was what we heard through the grapevine. Our sense was that they wondered if I would have purple hair, or wear leather and chains and have my body pierced in odd places, or have any idea how to handle children. They should have known Pat better than that, but then if she had gone off the deep end enough to become a lesbian, all bets were probably off.

I began my adult years as a Coast Guard officer's wife for God's sake, if anyone had cared enough to ask! Officers' wives learn early on not to dye their hair funny colors or wear leather and chains—it upsets the admirals. Officers' wives know from the time they say "I do" that their jobs are to raise model children, host perfect dinner parties, martyr their lives to their husbands' careers, and support the conservative sectors of the American government. Despite these restrictions, I managed to raise two magnificent daughters who have good manners, speak good English, and are caring, contributing members of society, if anyone had taken the time to find that out. They don't dye their hair purple either, and the additional piercing on one earlobe was done after that daughter left home.

———————

Well, the family arrived for lunch, and while they wrestled with what to say to one another and how to get the children to come out from behind their mother's skirts, I brought out a large bowl of colored rectangular wooden blocks. The trick with these blocks is to set them up in a row, winding in and out across the table, and up and down the little block steps. Once the pattern is finished, you simply tap the first block and they all fall like dominoes, round and round, up and down. I sat quietly with the big bowl of blocks and set them up, very slowly and carefully so as not to knock them down prematurely.

The grandchildren had gotten bold enough to sit on their Nana's lap. They watched me play from across the table until they could stand it no longer and had to get down off the lap to come see what I was doing. I didn't talk or make eye contact, and closer they came until they were standing by my side with big eyes, watching me set up those little blocks. You could have heard a pin drop as I put the last block in place, took a breath, and said to the children, "Would you like to tap it and see what happens?"

It was a good day. No one choked on lunch, and it seemed that I was to be trusted on a trial basis, for as they were leaving, the baby grabbed her sippy-cup full of pink lemonade, handed it to me and said, "This is yummy!" as she laughed and jumped in circles of sheer delight. A good day indeed.

At the Chiropractor

During the worst times of crises, when our shoulder blades were locked with muscle knots and our necks stopped rotating on command, we would visit the chiropractor. This has saved our lives. We went to an office where the doctors are kind, caring, and remembered our names, and where no one—even those who knew me two husbands ago—had blinked an eye when I showed up with Pat and explained how my life had changed. Except for one, who apparently wasn't in the loop. There came the unsuspecting visit when we emerged from our treatment sessions and went to the desk to pay. When this staff person read the insurance information and saw that Pat was a priest, you would have thought she had won the lottery the way she gushed and enthused! It turned out that *she* was very involved in *her* church (which was some variation on the Christian theme and sounded suspiciously fundamentalist), and it also turned out that she had one of those loud, overly-cheerful voices that shatters glass, destroys patient confidentiality, and does nothing for a freshly adjusted spine.

She engaged Pat—and the entire fully-occupied waiting room by association—in a lengthy monologue about religion, and I saw the whole finale laying itself out before my eyes as I fidgeted and tried to move us away from the front desk and out the door. Sure enough, when all had been said that could be covered without neglecting other patients, she looked at us brightly and said, "So, how do you two know each other?"

As protectively as I could, to spare Pat more trauma, I said (just as brightly), "We're partners!" Not missing a beat, she came back with: "That's wonderful. What do you *do*?"

I could have lied by omission. I could have explained that we run a small spiritual life center together and left it at that. We had our backs to about twenty-five people awaiting their sessions, and no one had to know. I could have escaped. But then I would have had to live with myself. So I said, "We're life partners; we're a *gay* couple."

Twenty-five people stop reading, or talking, or daydreaming, or chewing gum, and the deafening silence behind us was evenly matched by the speechlessness in front of us. Did we slink out the door? Were my feelings immediately identifiable? Do I remember anything of the ride home? Did we cry? Did we laugh? Does it ever end?

Church vs. State

The occasions on which the father of my children and I have to cross paths are mercifully few and far between. I'm sure he is as relieved about this as I am. There was the week my daughter had major surgery during her freshman year of college, and we all convened at a tiny hospital on the outskirts of Philadelphia—my "ex" and I sitting with her before she went into surgery, and our "wives" toughing it out upstairs in the waiting room. My daughter tormented the nursing staff by introducing her father's wife and her mother's female partner each as her "step-mother" and offering no explanation. I'm sure every one of those nurses chalked it up to the medication.

Then there was the high school graduation on a day so hot and steamy that Pat was considering wearing something light and comfortable in lieu of her clergy collar. "Will your 'ex' be wearing his uniform?" she asked me. "Absolutely," I replied. "Military officers always wear their uniforms for these kinds of occasions." "That's it then," she said with conviction. "This is church vs. state—I'm wearing my collar."

Every year the graduation guests are seated on the lawn facing a platform on one side of the high school building near the playing fields. Graduation is always scheduled for late afternoon in late May. The sun beats down on the assembled guests, then slowly sets behind the building, leaving the graduates and the speakers cooling off nicely in the shade and the guests squinting directly into the setting sun. This year was no exception. We sweltered and squinted and tried to take photographs with sweat dripping down our backs, steaming up our glasses, and wilting the programs in our hands. The temperature inside Pat's black "clericals" and under the stiff collar that is made of some fabric not found in nature had to be unthinkable, but she never twitched. She was the picture of composure in the chair next to me as my "ex," sitting across the aisle, leaned over to check us out.

We had hoped to escape at the end as soon as humanly possible, but a neighbor who had known us for years came running with her camera to get us ALL in a photograph—the graduate, her sister, *both* of her parents and *both* of their partners. "You are the only one of us who will want this picture on your refrigerator," I told her. Undeterred, she snapped the shot and left us alone—and there we all were, facing the challenge of small talk. You can only say, "Beautiful ceremony!", "Let me see those awards!", and "Cool diploma!" so many times. In public, my "ex" usually makes some manly, jocular comment intended for the company at large that barely conceals a jab about some failing of mine as a wife, mother, or human being. At which point I laugh it off to show that it's all in jest and there is really no discord between us, and walk away. I could see the glint in his eye and his expression starting, when Pat moved in to engage him in conversation. He mumbled something intended to simulate a polite response, looked at her collar, glanced at me, and backed off. This massive, uniformed six-foot-six-inch-tall military officer with a chest full of medals and no respect for women dropped his weapons when a five-foot-three-inch-short female priest saw what he was up to and intervened. For the first time in the history of our divorce, he didn't mess with me.

Never underestimate the power of religion.

I'm Not Gay Enough for That

Now I become myself. It's taken
Time, many years and places,
I have been dissolved and shaken,
Worn other people's faces . . .

Now there is time and Time is young.
O, in this single hour I live
All of myself and do not move
I, the pursued, who madly ran,
Stand still, stand still, and stop the Sun!

—May Sarton, *Now I Become Myself,* Collected Poems 1930-1973

Once Pat came out and lost her job, there was the looming question of how she was going to make a living. She had a few months of paid leave which was finally granted by the Episcopal Diocese after the Vestry of her church insisted it was the *least* that should be done for her. Because the Bishop had promised Pat that she would "never have another parish" as long as he was in office, she interviewed for college and hospital chaplaincy positions. Each interview was an agony of emotional turmoil as she wrestled with the question of whether to tell the interviewer, or interview committee, that she was gay. It boiled down to the choice between standing by her determination to be "out" and stay "out," and financial survival—for she knew beyond a doubt that being open about her homosexuality would cost her job opportunities, especially at Catholic hospitals and schools.

During this time, a friend invited Pat to participate in "guest preacher month" at the Congregational church in town. She agreed. The date was weeks away. By the time her Sunday arrived, however, she was in such a state of depression and despair that she begged me to call and cancel for her. When I refused, she had no choice but to get a sermon ready.

Pat had been given a tape of Arlo Guthrie's version of the hymn *Amazing Grace* by a colleague who had heard her story and said the song brought her to mind. Between the verses, Arlo narrates the story of the captain of an English slave ship, John Newton, who wrote *Amazing Grace*. On one of his trips to America with a ship full of African slaves, the captain looked at his human cargo and suddenly *saw* what he was doing. In the middle of the ocean, John Newton turned his ship around and took the slaves back home to Africa. Then he returned to England and spent the rest of his life writing spiritual hymns. *Amazing grace! How sweet the sound, that saved a wretch like me! I once was lost, but now am found; was blind, but now I see.* Here, Pat realized, was her sermon.

We arrived at church early the day she was to preach. I helped her on with her vestments and watched her kiss the stole, as priests do, before draping it over her shoulders. As she "robed," something began to happen. The color returned to her face. Her eyes regained their sparkle. The life-force energy that trauma and crisis had drained came back and was almost tangible.

When the time came, Pat walked down the aisle to the pulpit, and there she told the story of John Newton. She preached a sermon on what it is to "turn around for what we know is right," even if turning around goes against what the rest of the world *believes* is right. The congregation had no idea who Pat was, nor did they know the journey she was on, but they felt her passion, and you could have heard a pin drop as she sat back down and the organist played very softly, *Amazing Grace, how sweet the sound . . .*

The next morning over coffee Pat told me she had been talking to God. She realized, she said, that she was meant to be a parish priest, that the parish is where she comes alive, and that she really had no interest in working for a hospital or university. So she bargained with God: if God would find a way for her to serve a parish again, she would leave the Episcopal Church (remembering the Bishop's words) and change to whichever tradition she needed to change to: Congregational, Methodist, Presbyterian, or whatever. "Just *not* that MCC Church," she said to God. "I'm not gay enough for that."

Two hours (not two weeks or two months) later, the phone rang. Pat answered it upstairs and spoke for twenty minutes, then came downstairs with a strange look on her face. She said the call was from her new pastor friend at one of the local MCC Church's. He had decided to go back to Colorado, and was calling to ask if she had found a job yet, because if not, he would like to recommend her for the interim position at MCC.

Thus began her journey as a gay priest. As it turned out, she was exactly gay enough for that!

The MCC Fellowship

The Universal Fellowship of Metropolitan Community Churches (UFMCC) was started some thirty-five years ago by Rev. Troy Perry, who was thrown out of the Pentecostal Church as a young man for his homosexuality. "I began to share my dream for the church with the gay people I met," he explains in his book *The Lord is My Shepherd and He Knows I'm Gay.* "We had gone through generations, even centuries, of that awful conviction that if you were a homosexual you could not be a child of God; you could not be a Christian."[20] Twelve people attended the first service in Troy's living room in Huntington, California. Today there are Metropolitan Community Church (MCC) fellowships all over the world, some with *thousands* of members (would you believe, Texas?). Their churches have been burned to the ground; MCC ministers have been attacked and murdered; and Troy Perry has had to travel with bodyguards (as Gene Robinson eventually had to do) when touring the country to speak. But the UFMCC goes on. "I knew that I was not starting another Pentecostal church," Troy wrote. "I was starting a church that would be truly ecumenical . . . It would be a church that most could understand and easily identify with, and accept it as not being unusual or odd. It seemed to me that it should be traditional, almost like those (Catholic, Episcopal and churches of various Protestant sects) they attended in childhood.[21]

———

Pat was allowed to retain "good standing" as a priest in the Episcopal Diocese of Connecticut when she came out as a lesbian, was dismissed from her parish and found herself without employment. But that "good standing" was all she retained. The church—bishops, clergy friends and colleagues—simply vanished into the woodwork. Only *one* pastoral phone call was made to see how things were going, and that was to Pat's soon-to-be ex-husband. The sense we got in 1998 was that Pat was too "hot" to be associated with; no one wanted to be seen supporting her until they found out just which way the winds of church policy were going to blow. The "openly gay clergy group" which gave us such initial inspiration turned out to be ineffectual—no one really wanted to come out! The bishop wavered in his interaction with the group, and it died after several meetings.

Two life-saving exceptions to the lack of pastoral understanding and care need special recognition. They were Pat's spiritual director, The Rev. Ted Coolidge (retired), and the (then) Rev. Canon Gene Robinson of New Hampshire, who at the time of this writing has become the first openly-gay bishop and is now either the most famous bishop in the world next to Desmond Tutu, or, "the most dangerous man in the Church," depending upon who you talk to. Both of these men listened supportively as Pat told her story, and both encouraged her to follow her path while the Church pretended she didn't exist. In many ways they were her angels.

I have never been a church-goer, and Pat was in hiding, so it surprised us both when someone told us about the MCC and I had the intuitive sense that we should go. So clear was this sense that I became adamant, with the result that for several weeks we went to church twice on Sundays: morning worship at MCC Hartford and afternoon worship at MCC New Haven.

The day Pat and I attended our first MCC service, we arrived at a beautiful little chapel that was streaming with light and full of people just like us. Even before we got to the door Pat said, "I can feel God here." By the time the sermon was halfway through that morning, Pat was crying so hard she had to leave the room, and my tears were splashing onto the hymnal and blinding me. We heard about a young gay man who had been beaten and whose attackers had carved the word "faggot" into the skin on his back. We heard about hatred, and about love. We heard preaching that transformed us, in the only church where I have ever felt remotely at ease. Communion at MCC is unusual among churches, for it is a welcoming, open experience where all seekers are invited; no one is excluded. We received the bread and the wine, then approached the minister for a personal blessing. We went as a couple. He listened to our concerns, put his hands on our shoulders and offered a prayer. At the end we kissed—him, and each other, and returned to our seats. We sang the Holly Near hymn: *We are a gay and lesbian people—and we are singing, singing for our lives . . .*

That afternoon we attended another MCC service. We watched gay couples enter the sanctuary holding hands or carrying their children. We saw gay sons and daughters bringing their heterosexual parents, siblings, and friends to the service with them. We stood in a circle for communion, feeding one another the bread and the wine, holding hands for the blessing. For the first time in my life I saw the humanity in that circle as beautiful sisters and brothers. All of them: the stereotypical gorgeous gay boys and tough lesbians, the heterosexuals who weren't afraid to be with us, the homosexuals you would never guess were homosexual, the cross-dressers, the priests and organists (Episcopal and Catholic) who had served their own churches in the morning and come to worship where they could be "out" in the afternoon, and the transsexual—the most courageous of us all. These people were *real*. In this church, they had nothing to lose, and nothing to hide. This church was *really* about love and acceptance for everyone. It was honest and "clean"—no hypocrisy, no deception, no judgment, no "pseudo-Christianity." And we sang:

> *Surely the presence of our God is in this place—*
> *I can feel thy mighty power, and thy grace.*
> *I can hear the brush of angel's wings,*
> *I see Glory on each face—*
> *Surely, the presence, of our God is in this place.*

Pat became the interim minister of MCC New Haven within a year. The Episcopal Church is not "in communion" with the MCC, of course, and she should never have applied for the job, but she hoped no one would notice in the commotion of electing a new bishop. A year later Pat's interim time at MCC was drawing to a close. Interim pastors cannot apply for the permanent position, but people were begging her to stay and—with no prospect of another parish position within her own church—she considered leaving the Episcopal church and entering the process to become an MCC minister. Meanwhile a new Episcopal bishop was elected to the Diocese of Connecticut. He called Pat to a meeting, where she expected to be reprimanded, if not expelled from the church. Instead the new bishop said, "I know where you've been, and why you had to go. Would you be willing to come back home?" Perhaps, she thought, by returning as an "out" priest in a traditional church, taking with her all she had learned, she could help to change the world—or at least the Church. She agreed to return.

The Children

*Now more than ever, we need to mend what needs heal-
ing in all our relationships . . . Now more than ever, we
need to be the peace that we seek, and live what we want
for our children.*

—Louise Diamond, *The Peace Book*

By the time Pat and I got together I was at the stage of
parenthood where you see the light at the end of the
tunnel: the day when all of the children will be off to college and life can become quiet and contemplative. I knew
Pat had grandchildren with whom she was very close, but
hadn't focused on what this actually meant, logistically, in
terms of our living together. It was news to me, for example,
that once a week two of the grandchildren spent the night
with her, and that she wanted to keep this up as long as she
could—for her sake, and for theirs. "Overnight?" I said.
"In *this* house?" "I thought I was *finished* with diapers and
teething, and whining children, and high chairs, and sticky
fingers all over the furniture, and getting up all night long
because someone wants a drink of water, or has wet the
bed, or is scared of the dark," I said.

Pat is a flexible, easy-going person, but on the issue of
her grandchildren there was no talking to her. There was
much too much turmoil in their lives caused by her leaving their grandfather for her to cause more by changing
routines, she said. And that was that.

So the children came to visit; two the first year, two more
the next, and then—without anyone consulting me—five
new grandchildren were conceived and brought into the

world! We collected high chairs and booster seats, blow-up beds, and baby blankets. We brought out the baskets of toys I had in the basement. We figured out what each child liked in particular—this one loved puzzles, and this one was learning to read, and this one was the artist, and this one would play board games all day long, and this one loved animals and being outdoors, this one liked to snuggle and this one had to be approached slowly, this one went right to bed and this one had to be rocked to sleep, and this little piggy went to market . . . and my hardened heart began to melt.

It didn't matter that overlapping grandchildren were being toilet-trained the same year. It didn't matter about the dirty diapers and the accidents, and the spills and the sticky fingers; it didn't matter how appalled my teenagers were to find training pants mixed in with their Victoria Secret underwear, or that my 19-year-old regressed to the point of a shouting match with a pre-schooler about who controlled the TV channels (were they going to watch Barney, or the UNH hockey game?); it didn't matter how many times a three-year-old asked the same question, or how many yolks a six-year-old broke trying to fry her own egg, or how many sibling battles we broke up as they turned Legos into lethal weapons. It didn't matter how shocked my family was to see me arrive with not one, but two baby car seats in the back of my car, and it didn't matter how many times we held a newborn. Each one was a miracle of new life, as awe-inspiring as the last one we held. This was love.

We established rituals: the "sacred baths" (which a four-year-old called "secret baths"), where the child had the tub to her/himself with essential oils added to the water, music playing, and lights lowered, the brushing of hair and the rubbing of lotion on dry legs and arms, the bedtime stories and games, the candles we lit at dinner which they took turns blowing out at the end of the meal, the table manners I absolutely had to put into writing and read before meals until the older ones could read them for us: "Dinner is a time for sitting and talking quietly while sharing a meal together. Getting up and down from the table, banging the silverware, running your fork through the candle flame, kicking your sibling, complaining about what is served, spitting out food and arguing are neither appropriate nor acceptable. Napkins go in the lap and are not to be put back on the table, no matter how dirty they are, until dinner is over . . ." And so on.

We became a household stocked with extra socks, underwear, and sweat-shirts; diaper-rash ointment, Snoopy band-aids, and tear-free shampoo, tapes of children's lullabies, sticker books for good behavior, and closets filled with gifts for every occasion. We bought a new camera and created a wall gallery of children's photos. I took up knitting again.

Pat's part of the deal was just as shocking, for she had to live with a teenager's room where the mess was beyond description, phone and computer lines tied up, boyfriends arriving day and night whether we were dressed and functioning or not, curfew battles, white-knuckle rides with a learner's permit ("I'll do the baby diapers if you teach the 16-year-old to drive," we agreed), prom night hysteria and generalized sullenness, ear-splitting stereos, the slamming of doors, and the constant smell of horse gear that never got stored in the proper place. She would look at me with panic in her eyes and say, "I thought I was *finished* with teenagers!" as she picked her way around the saddles and bridles spread out to be cleaned on the living room floor.

We fell into our respective roles: I am the disciplinarian, the no-nonsense, follow the rules, buckle your seatbelt, don't stand up in your high chair, make eye contact when you shake people's hands, and behave-yourself kind of adult. Bedtime is bedtime; sugar will ruin your teeth; TV is an outrage; computer games numb the psyche; good grammar is imperative (the English language is fraught with irregular verbs and complicated past tenses which if not mastered young are not mastered at all); and if there is no nighttime bath, a hot washcloth on hands and face is a minimum. Pat is the compassionate one; she knows how to have fun, will buy treats, play games, bend rules, relax curfews, mediate conflict, and extend bedtimes. We make the perfect team.

Loving the children as a couple means that our relationship goes far beyond ourselves. If we don't stay true to who we are; if we don't stay honest; if we don't simply raise the children and love the grandchildren together to the best of our ability just like anyone else, then we let them all down. Who else in the family is as qualified to address the questions that come, inevitably, anywhere between the ages of five and seven? Who better than we to take on this dialogue?:

Nana, do you two kiss like married people do?
Yes, we do!
Then who's the boy, and who's the girl?

Who else, when they ask "Why do you live with Karen, Nana?" could explain as clearly as we can about our love for one another, about homosexuality and the words "gay" or "lesbian" and what they mean and how some of the rest of the world thinks about it and why? Who else is going to fully understand when a grandson talks about being teased on the school bus because he is "different?"

This book is for the children. We're working around the clock to create a world where they will not have to work their way through the pain toward hope of the promise; a world which will welcome all of them for who they are, no matter what that looks like.

Gay Youth

Gay and lesbian youth are two to three times more likely to attempt suicide than their heterosexual counterparts . . . How many suicides in our churches by young men and women have really been caused by the homophobia of the Church?

—Marilyn B.Alexander & James Preston, *We Were Baptized Too*

While some lesbians and gay men grow up with no religious bonding, many of those who do come to feel like abandoned children. When they look to their religions for affirmation of their inherent goodness, and a viable pathway to a Creator, they often come away empty-handed. They find that Mother Church and Father God have deserted them, purportedly attending to other wayward children while making it clear that gay sons and daughters are to be considered virtual nonmembers of their ecclesial families. This abandonment can undo the spiritual life image of gays and lesbians, leaving them feeling homeless, deserted, unloved, rejected, unlovable, shamed, and enraged . . .

—Craig O'Neill and Kathleen Ritter, *Coming Out Within*

June, 2002

Dear Bishop, Pat wrote:

In a recent conversation about the Bishop's 2004 Conference on Children and Youth, I asked how the Conference planned to address the particular problems of gay youth. No one had an answer. So I volunteered to help.

At the Planning Team Meeting in Hartford, I heard that the

Diocese would like to get 'more people involved' in planning the Conference. It occurred to me that we might want to identify the gay youth in our parishes, and encourage them to participate in the planning. I spoke with several people about having a retreat day for gay youth in the Diocese in order to get to know who they are, and was told we needed your permission.

Today I received a phone call with the message that you wouldn't endorse a gathering for gay youth at this time because you want to 'be sensitive' to the 'issues,' and you don't want to 'put this in the face of people right now.'

Your reaction causes me deep concern and immediately brings to mind the 'it's OK to be gay, just don't shove it in our faces' attitude that homosexuals hear with depressing regularity from people who call themselves 'tolerant.'

I strongly believe that the Church has the highest moral obligation to make amends to homosexuals for the psychological and spiritual damage it has caused them. I can't tell you the number of gay people I've counseled whose deepest wounding comes not from their families, or society at large, but from the Church. Remember, the words 'sin,' 'perversion,' and 'abomination' originate within the Church. If there is sensitivity to be had, it would be to homosexuals, not to their oppressors! Gay youth exist— probably many more than we know—and all the 'sensitivity' in the world to those who don't want to hear about it doesn't change that.

Homosexuality in the church is one of the biggest issues of the day, next to the threat of war. (Indeed, the two become one when religious leaders use battle cries in their 'war' against gay people). It needs to be confronted and addressed, for churches around the world are beginning to tear themselves apart over this issue. Gay youth in our Diocese will see that gay priests are coming out of the closet, that openly gay people are being ordained as priests (and now bishops!), that the State of Connecticut gets ever closer to legalizing 'gay marriage, and that the new Archbishop of Canterbury has publicly supported homosexuals in the church.

How can we honor and help to heal these young people if we don't know who they are? I assume you are aware of the statistic reflecting the fact that the highest population at risk for suicide is gay youth.[22] Somehow we need to get to know these children and to hear their stories. Everyone needs to hear their stories. Somehow the gay kids need to be encouraged to come to the Conference and participate as young people who are welcomed for who they are. If they don't come they will remain 'children of the shadows,'[23] and the wounding will go on, and on, and on.

Given the tenor of the times, I find it extremely disconcerting that you are not ready to organize or publicize an event in support of the gay youth in our Diocese. I'm willing to create a program for them at a location of your choice, and will work with anyone who wants to help. I hope this letter will enable you to rethink your decision and give me the permission I need to proceed. I await your reply on this critical matter.

Yours in Christ,

Pat+

The Bishop's Conference on Youth was held in March of 2004. The gay issue was never addressed.

Good News

If we are truly going to live at peace in our local and global communities, we need to get over these arbitrary divisions and learn to live together in harmony. We will have to remember that our unity as a single family of life on this Earth, and our wonderful diversity within that unity, are but two sides of the same coin.

—Louise Diamond, *The Peace Book*

D*ear Editor*, Pat wrote:

I am writing in response to the article, 'New Plan Offers Episcopal Oversight to Conservative Parishes,' in the April/May 2002 issue of Good News.

I was shocked to hear of the endorsement by the House of Bishops in Camp Allen, Texas of a plan to allow conservative parishes (defined here as those who object to the 'pushing of homosexuality and women's ordination against their will') to 'seek oversight (supervision) from like-minded bishops outside their dioceses.' A group of twenty conservative bishops said that failure to approve the new agreement would 'lead to a season of loss, lawlessness, litigation, and intervention,' and called the approval of the decision 'a significant act of grace . . .'

I am an openly-gay female Episcopal priest. To think that my ordination and my sexuality so offend my conservative colleagues that simply being asked to accept who I am would lead them to 'lawlessness and litigation' saddens me beyond words. There is nothing Christ-like about 'lawlessness and litigation.'

The article explains that church leaders now believe 'co-existing at arms' length' (between liberal and conservative Episco-

palians) is a sign of strength, not weakness. 'Co-existing at arms' length . . .' Is this what Jesus would have done? Is this how we plan to promote love and peace among ourselves and within the world? How can we be so blind?

I believe that we live in a civilization based on a twisted compromise of Jesus' teachings, and that much of the Church has followed suit. Jesus was about love. End of discussion.

Respectfully submitted,

Rev. Patricia Gallagher

Coming Home

During the turbulent years of my second heterosexual marriage, there were times when I had to take my children and leave the house for the night, or a few days, until their step-father's violent, bipolar-driven rages subsided. A woman who was just becoming a friend during the worst stage of my unraveling life told me she had an upstairs guest suite that her tenant had vacated; I could use it anytime, she said. Within a week of her invitation, I called her to say we were coming.

My daughters were quiet and well-behaved. Shellshocked. We got them settled into the queen-size bed in the guest room, then sat down for an adult dinner and conversation. She cooked a gourmet meal which we ate sitting cross-legged on cushions pulled up to the living room coffee table. She lit candles and served wine. I told her about my marriage until I was too exhausted to say any more, and it was time for sleep. She looked at me and said, "It will be awfully crowded for you in that bed with your kids. Why don't you sleep in my bed with me?"

The fact that she slept with her three Springer Spaniels was only part of what stopped me cold and made me stammer an excuse, thanking her anyway. Women share beds all the time—sisters, room mates, friends, cousins. Besides, I love dogs, so what was the problem? The "problem" was that something registered in my psyche. An awareness clicked into place that terrified me on the one hand ("Why would she want me to sleep in her bed?" I kept asking myself. "We hardly know each other"), and on the other hand left me wondering for months what it would have been like if I *had* slept in her bed. Something was pulling at me, which I couldn't explain.

Early in my first marriage before we had children, I found racquetball and squash partners in every town that had courts. By great good fortune, one of my female partners was a racquetball coach and was willing to play with me once or twice a week. That's all we did together. Not much conversation, no lunch and coffee afterwards, not even a sauna together. But my husband was jealous. "Why do you have to spend so much time with her?" he would say. "Do you have to play *every* week?" I couldn't for the life of me figure out what was upsetting him—this woman and I weren't even friends! Looking back I see that she was clearly lesbian. My husband picked that up and didn't want me around her, because somewhere in the recesses of his mind, he suspected that I was too.

Moving backward through my life, there was the train trip I took with my boyfriend from the south of France to Florence, Italy at the age of nineteen. I struck up a conversation with a woman in the aisle as we were putting our luggage in the overhead compartment some distance from my seat. We talked ten minutes or so, and then she asked bluntly, "Are you gay?" "No!" I protested too loudly. "My boyfriend is sitting right over there." (This was a precursor to the mantra so many of us have adopted while swirling in the confusion of our denial: "I can't be gay, I'm married"). I returned to my seat and related the conversation to my male companion. "Why on earth do you think she would ask me if I were gay?" I asked him. "Europeans are like that," he replied, to my great relief.

Growing up, I had two close friends all through grammar school. We went to three different high schools and lost touch with one another—until my senior year of high school, when one of them, an artist, sent me a book she had drawn and narrated that was completely about me. The drawings revealed the time we had spent together as children, the jokes we had shared and the games we had played. The narrative extolled my virtues—how funny and bright and athletic I was. Something registered. Something felt strange. Why would she create this book about me years after we had lost contact with one another? I felt uneasy as I thanked her for the book by phone.

During my senior year of college the other grammar school friend called me out of the blue. I don't even know how she found me. I was surprised to hear her voice, and even more surprised when she invited me to Cape Cod for the weekend! Floating way in the back of my consciousness, almost not accessible, was a running conversation with myself as we talked on the phone: "There was always something 'hidden' about her, something mysterious that I couldn't put my finger on. I wonder if she's lesbian and just coming out. I wonder if she thinks we could be lovers because we knew each other so well as children. I wonder if that's why she is inviting me to spend a weekend with her." On the face of it, old friends re-connect all the time. There's nothing strange or frightening about that. This, however, felt strange and frightening and I couldn't explain why. I made excuses not to go and promised to keep in touch, which I never did. For years, in the back of my mind almost out of reach, I imagined what our reconnecting would have meant.

Then there were the pre-adolescent years. At ten or

eleven years old, role playing was the big game: Cops and robbers, cowboys and Indians, mother and father, doctor and nurse, "lost" children. I played the male roles. One day we enacted a story taken directly from TV where, in the end, the man throws the woman onto the bed, jumps on top of her and kisses her. We were very convincing right up to the kiss, when I pushed the girl playing the woman onto the floor, jumped on top of her, and kissed her on the lips. For longer than I had expected. A few seconds, in fact. We were old enough to become embarrassed, so I jumped back up and we went on to another game. But I never forgot that kiss. I never forgot how my whole body tingled; how it felt warm, natural and right. Thirty-five years worked their way through my life before I had that feeling again.

"A woman knows what a woman needs," is what they say. "Lesbian love is the most beautiful love in the world," they say. I understood the general concept, but was skeptical about anything beyond that. I wondered right along with the people who said, "What, exactly, do lesbians *do*?" I didn't start examining my sexuality until half-way through a second marriage, when I knew for damned sure that I was finished living with men; finished with the emotional strain, tension and confusion that, for me, had always accompanied that "life-style." Living alone would be an enormous relief, I thought.

At some unidentifiable point, the little sentence, "Maybe you're meant to be with a woman," starting creeping into my awareness. I ignored it, thinking I was just grasping at straws. But the idea took hold, and wasn't straw-like at all. It grew and expanded and began to define how I saw the world; it allowed me to breathe. It made sense. Pieces came crashing into place. I remembered attractions to women I hadn't known were attractions: the high school classmate whose beautiful hands I couldn't take my eyes off of through every history class, the friend whose bathing-suit-clad-body turned my insides upside down at the pool and I thought it must be heartburn, the female college friend from whom I was inseparable. The song *Have You Ever Really Loved a Woman* was a radio favorite that year and it sang to every part of my unrealized self. I began to "feel" the female partner I would someday meet, and my heart almost burst with joy. Two and a half years passed this way before we met, and for six months we interacted with one another only as friends. Even after we were free to become lovers, I was afraid to approach her.

What should I do?

Where would we begin?

When the time came, I looked into her eyes, touched her face, and dared to put my lips to hers. The rest was simply coming home.

The Dream

And then the day came when the risk to remain tight in a bud was more painful than the risk it took to blossom.

— Anais Nin

People have asked why I had no trouble coming out, and my ready answer has always been: "because I wasn't raised in the church."

"And my father is gay," I would add, as if this were of secondary importance. Perhaps I need to revisit this, for had my father not broken the legacy of an entrenched, southern, Presbyterian, puritanical upbringing (which he did in part by hitch-hiking north for a summer job after college and never going back), he would likely never have come out. Had he never come out, I might have carried the full weight of the suffocating, repressive values and standards that are technically my birthright, and I, too, might still be in the closet.

On religion, my father wrote in his memoirs at the age of 80: *I was brought up to be a 'good' boy, and was sent to Sunday school as soon as I was able to go; I said my prayers every night until I was in college and struggled unsuccessfully to read the Bible in German. By the age of 11 or 12 when I could play the piano well enough to play hymns, I was pressed into service every Sunday morning and every Sunday night at 'Christian Endeavor' . . . The Hunters, being of Scottish descent, were naturally Presbyterians . . . Our Presbyterian church was a dismal architectural nightmare, and I can still smell the basement where we went for Daily Vacation Bible School. The Rev. Dr. Henderlight was a tall elderly man who wore a swallowtail morn-*

*ing coat and a stiff high collar. He preached Hell and damnation
. . .*

On his mother's view of sex: *She made it emphatic that there are certain things that one simply cannot talk about, so the silence about such things as sex screamed louder than any amount or kind of talk. When I moved to Connecticut in 1941 and made friends with a wonderful musician/singer, one day she said that there is nothing one can't talk about. Nothing? It was as though someone had unlocked a door, or had opened a window, or had turned on the light. Mama's training had created such an emotional block in me that I am amazed that, as sexually inhibited as I was, I survived, married and had children.*

By the time I was born, my father had rejected both the church and puritanical attitudes toward sex. He married, had five children with whom he was willing to discuss anything but God, and lived what appeared to be the most normal of heterosexual lives. Until a dream woke him up to another reality:

I had a significant dream, he wrote: *It was a very pleasant but disturbing dream, and the moment I woke up I knew that my life would never be the same. I had to face the fact that I had just had my first completely-remembered homoerotic dream: no sexual activity—just sleeping with a man. The implications were frightening; I assumed that my marriage would not survive, that my home and family would be lost and that I would ultimately be disgraced. I panicked.*

I dreaded appearing at breakfast for fear every detail of the dream would be written all over my face and would be read with shock and condemnation by my wife and children. Mercifully they were oblivious—how could they know? —but I still had an enormous sense of guilt.

This was the beginning as he remembers it, and it was only the beginning. What ensued was the inevitable painful and exhilarating process of fully coming to grips with his homosexuality—and then there was a thirty-year marriage to bring to a close. In the end, I was the first of his children to whom my father came out, probably because I am the oldest, and in good linear fashion he worked his way down the line. My father had come to live with my husband and me after separating from my mother, and we were at the dinner table one night. *I agonized about how to do it,* he wrote, *but finally organized and rehearsed my speech over and over. One night after dinner, I said: 'Ahem,' or something like that and told them I had something to discuss with them. They looked up—and waited, and waited—and waited. I was paralyzed.*

My son-in-law said: 'Well, you have our attention.' All my rehearsed lines were completely lost, and I couldn't remember a word. After a ghastly silence, I blurted out something, but I don't remember what it was. The truth somehow spilled out . . .

He's going to tell us he's dying, I had thought. He's going to say he has a terminal, or a lingering, wasting disease. I had never seen my strong, articulate, in-command, father look as vulnerable. And I had never seen him begin to speak and then become frozen. In that wordless silence, I was beginning to panic. What could this be? His whole body looked vulnerable, but it was the eyes that made me think he was going to announce something so serious, so frightening, that it must be about death. I've seen eyes like that since, always in gay men (for a patriarchy, I believe, is harder on gay men than it is on lesbians)—that mixture of archetypal fear and impossible hope. It's a pleading, trapped look, reflecting a need (to be accepted) that might never be met: a look that says, "I have no choice but to say this because it's the truth—but as I speak, I'm well aware that I may be crucified for what I say."

I remember *exactly* what my father said that night at the dinner table, when he finally could speak. He said, "I've realized . . ." and then he stopped for a long time, "that I am homosexual." He had his face almost buried in his hands but was still looking at us. There *was* shock, and my mouth *did* drop open for a number of seconds—this was something I never could have predicted. It removed one way of knowing my father and replaced it with another; it took a while to sink in. When it did sink in and I realized that he was merely gay and not dead or dying, my relief was so great that he could have told me he was also a cross-dresser and it wouldn't have made any difference. There was no condemnation.

Why, I don't really know. Perhaps because I had been raised to believe my father was the voice of truth, that he was always right. If he said he was homosexual, who was I to argue or judge?

Gay people universally talk about having felt "different" all their lives, and are often horrified to have to admit that their "difference" is about their sexual orientation. If and when they come out, the gay label leaves them feeling more ostracized from mainstream society than ever—in other words, still "different" with the additional burden of a label that makes them potential targets of hatred and intolerance. I, too, have always felt "different," but when I finally figured out why, I was relieved beyond description to know that there was, after all, a category to which I belonged! Family! Sisters and brothers of my own kind! This was nothing but good news to me, and I have the sneaking suspicion that my joy was possible because the trail had been blazed before me, a trail that started with my father's dream.

Sexuality

In many ancient cultures, gays and lesbians were not the objects of sexual projection, at least not in the negative sense. Native Americans call gays the "two-spirited people," meaning that they have both male and female spirits. Gays and lesbians were often seen as specifically blessed, not specifically cursed, as it were; 'double' people rather than 'half a man' or 'half a woman.'

—Nancy Wilson, *Our Tribe*

A great weariness comes over me living at this time in history because I see how blind we are and how far we have to go before we become clear about our sexuality. The sexual problems of our culture begin and end, of course, with a legacy of sexual repression that originated, by common consensus, with the fifth-century philosopher and theologian Augustine, Bishop of Hippo. Here's where we got into trouble: "Prior to his baptism, Augustine had identified himself with the school of Manichaean philosophy, which accepted a radical dualism about human life. The Manichaeans tended to divide human life somewhere about the diaphragm, pronouncing the lower body parts evil and the higher body parts good. Augustine, in his pre-Christian days, had lived out of wedlock with his lover, by whom he had produced a son. His conversion led him to renounce his flesh, abandon his lover and their child, and take up the 'higher calling' of a Christian ascetic, ultimately becoming a priest and bishop . . . His primary spiritual task was to remove the stain of his sexual desire. He thus became the great theologian of guilt and sin, but, as is so often the case, he remained blind to the price that others had to pay for his righteousness. Evil, the sin in life, was for Augustine located in the flesh. It was transmitted through sex."[24]

To this day our understanding of the way things are, as "Christians," is based upon the illusion that anything involving the body is at best a threat and at worst the work of the devil—the expression of feelings (particularly passion), pleasurable bodily sensations (particularly ecstasy), and sexuality (which we reduce to *sex*). We are supposed to "know" God from the neck up, with our "higher" selves, and pretend that everything below the neck, which represents our "lower, animal-like" selves, doesn't exist. Copulation is to produce offspring, and the body is to be used as a "workhorse"—pain is to be denied, pleasure kept to a minimum. If it feels good, it's a sin. Don't explore sexuality; don't find out who you are; just choose an opposite-gender partner with whom to mate in the missionary position for the purpose of having children, and get on with your life. While the rest of the world understands that the purpose of sexual energy is to have it flow from the heart, we Americans in particular are stuck at the genitals, with the tragic results displayed (flaunted) throughout our culture.

Author Thomas Moore states in his introduction to *The Soul of Sex*: "It's clear to me that sex is one of the most important aspects of human life, second perhaps only to religion, and these are often inseparable . . . in some ways, sex is the facade of the soul, and when we deal with it thoughtfully, the whole interior cosmos comes into the foreground."[25] "Sexuality and spirituality are inseparable," author Christian de la Huerta says in his book *Coming Out*

Spiritually. ". . . when sexuality was split from the sacred, the missionary position between man and woman became the only acceptable form of sex, and any behavior that deviated from that was deemed a 'waste of seed,' shameful, and morally reprehensible . . ." *Erotic energy is powerful, sacred, and universal. It is creative and transformative. It is the same as the universal forces of creation, which cause flowers to bloom in sensual displays of color, texture, and scent; which cause volcanoes to erupt and generate new land masses; and which give birth to new, unimaginable star systems. We live in a sexual universe.*[26] Our sexuality is our life force; you mess with that, and you mess with the core of who we are. Peoples' lives, and by extension society at large, can be (and often are) entirely shaped by sexual wounding.

How did we come so far astray?

———

I heard a lesbian friend say the other day, "I think people can be gay and not know it." She said this as if it were a revelation. I wanted to scream at her, "Of COURSE people can be gay and not know it! Haven't most of us been gay and not known it, except the lucky few who have always known? If you look around, wouldn't it seem to be true that the majority of gay people don't know that they're gay?" How could they know? Are there any of us whose parents said, when we were children: *When you come into your sexuality, you will begin to get a sense of who you are. There are several ways your sexuality can manifest, and there are many ways to love; you may want to be with someone of your own gender, or you may want to be with someone of the opposite gender, or you may feel drawn to both. Pay attention to your heart;*

pay attention to what calls you and where you feel most comfortable; pay attention to who attracts you and where you feel at home?

Did any of us receive this message, or even minimal information, about the possibility of being gay? Did we have even remote modeling that it was OK to be gay or that being homosexual was normal, natural, and simply different (not better, not worse) from being heterosexual? Even I, whose father came out after thirty years of marriage and five children, used to say to myself, "Since my father is gay, I wonder if any of his children are too . . ." And I would survey my siblings with a critical eye. Now that I'm the one who is out, I look at the faded black and white photograph of my kindergarten class picture and notice that I am the girl in the group who is indistinguishable from the boys. I've always looked "boy-like." I've always *felt* "boy-like." If only I could have received the message: "You're fine. Boy-like is beautiful!"

I have a few theories, which my family and friends are tired of hearing. My first theory is that for every gay person in a family there are others—often many others. Like for every brown-haired member of a family there are others, or people with freckles, or people with dimples in the chin, or people who tend to put on weight. I am convinced that homosexuality is a genetic trait. Many people join me in believing this to be true, yet very few of my openly gay friends will consider the possibility that they have family members who "might" be gay. My theory is, try to find the few members of a gay person's family who are *not* gay! The openly gay people I know seem to think they are the only ones. They seem to think of themselves as an aberration, an abnormality, a birth defect (which supports the genetic theory), a "problem," a "disgrace" to their families, a "sinner" whom God will never love, or at the very least "the only one." Where do these people think we come from? Do they think we simply develop in a vacuum from heterosexual parents with no plausible explanation? That we emerge out of nowhere, to enter the world for the purpose of living in hiding and shame for most of our lives? These gay people who think they are the only ones struggle to come out, sometimes to no one but themselves and a few intimate friends, sometimes to all of their friends but not their families, sometimes to family and friends but not to colleagues at work. Those of us who live and breathe it know very well about the many levels and layers—and daily decisions around—"coming out."

Because gay people so often believe themselves to be the "only ones" in their families, their journeys are that much lonelier, especially in families horrified by the concept of homosexuality. We have a friend whose two sisters—the people she is closest to in the world—have told her that they consider homosexuals to be "*on a par with murderers*." It is hardly surprising, then, that she has never come out to them. The fact is, if we really look at our parents, aunts, uncles, cousins, nieces and nephews, grandparents, siblings, and children, we'll see that we (gay people) are, indeed, everywhere within our family trees. Now that my "gaydar" is razor sharp, I look at the families of every gay person whose family I know, or simply at family photos, and the truth stares me right in the face. We are not the only ones!

Pat and I spoke with a handsome young college man

about his "coming out," which was new and very difficult for him. The first thing he told us was, *I finally had to admit that I'm gay—I fit every stereotype! I'm a 'mamma's boy,' I tap dance, I'm majoring in theatre, I've always known that I was 'different'—and, I'm in love with a man!* I asked if he thought he was the "only one" in his family. He said, *Absolutely. I'm the only one. And I could never tell my mother or grandmother—it would destroy them.* I said, "Are you *sure* you're the only one? *Think about it.*" He was quiet for a minute, and then he said, "Well, I've always wondered about my grandmother, and my friends all say that my sister is clearly a lesbian, and my mother once confided to me that she never liked having sex with my father, and then there's my aunt . . ." Imagine how much less agony this young man would have suffered if it was so "OK" to be gay in our society that the other gay members of his family could also have come out!

I heard one lesbian say that her mother refused to acknowledge her lesbianism and would be appalled if she chose to "marry" a same-sex partner. Yet the woman's mother has "no problem" with the fact that her brother has been married seven times! Could this brother have been married seven times because he's barking up the wrong tree? Even though heterosexual marriage hasn't worked for him, both he and his mother believe that at least he is doing it "right" and the lesbian would be doing it "wrong." Here, in a nutshell, is the tragic misconception that causes untold, and unnecessary, human agony.

Theory number two is that gay people often marry gay people. I mean into "heterosexual" marriages. Since so many of us don't know we're gay, or we know at some level but won't "go there" because it's "wrong" and "per-verted," or we know but we very much want to have children, we find each other in the opposite sex. Gay energy attracts gay energy. Perhaps it is because gay men are attracted to the masculine in the lesbian, and the lesbian is attracted to the feminine in the gay man, or simply that we recognize each other and feel at home together. Whatever. I see these couples everywhere, over and over again—gay men and lesbian women married to one another. Sometimes their misery is so obvious that they have the aura of caged animals about them. Often, however (very often), they talk about their love for one another, about the fact that they feel like "soul mates," about how they have always been "best friends"—and I think I must be mistaken about my theory. And then I get a little closer and hear that they have always felt more like brother and sister than lovers. I notice the alcoholism or drug abuse hidden within that relationship, or that every one of the wife's friends is an "out" lesbian, or that she spends all of her time with her "women friends" (whom I know are lesbian) and that the husband prefers the "housewife" role, staying home to cook, take care of the kids, and decorate the house. I'll hear the wife say, for example, "My husband has always been my best friend, but I've never been interested in sex, so we don't sleep together much," or, "I had an affair with a woman, but that was when (and only because) I was drinking (or taking drugs), and now I'm trying to make my marriage work." In the scenarios that end realistically, I hear that one of the couple has "run off" with a same-sex partner, and I pray that the other one eventually does the same. You'd be amazed at how many lesbians have come out, partnered with a woman, and then said of their ex-husbands, "I know he's gay, but he'll never figure it out."

So, let me ask the obvious question: What do we think the chances are that marriages between closeted lesbians and gay men will produce one or more gay children? About 100 per cent maybe? *That's* were we all come from! In the book *The Man Jesus Loved*, which theologian Ted Jennings of Chicago Theological Seminary was outrageously courageous enough to publish in 2003, Jennings quotes Austrian psychoanalyst Georg Walther Groddeck who, in the late 1800's, discussed the theme of homosexuality that he took to be *basic* to human affectional life. "Groddeck," Jennings quotes, (emphasis mine) "finds modern Western culture's ignorance of the *primacy* of homosexuality to be astonishing, as if willful ignorance prevented the West from seeing what is right before its eyes."[27] I rest my case.

Theory number three is that the people most violently opposed to homosexuality are themselves the most deeply "closeted" homosexuals. This theory is not new or original; it is shared by anyone who understands the psychology of repression, denial, and projection, the psychology of the un-claimed "shadow." To quote Thomas Moore quoting Sigmund Freud: "We display outrageously and obsessively that which we do not fully possess or have deeply at our disposal."[28] My heart aches when I attend marches, rallies, and legislative hearings for gay rights, and I see the almost universally closeted "opposition"—red in the face, foaming at the mouth, rigid in rhetoric and adamant in the stance that homosexuality is an "abomination." I stay quiet and breathe deeply, trying to change the energy in the crowd to compassion while sending the message again and again: "It's OK to be gay. It's OK to come out. It's OK."

Until we make this normal, until we all come out of hiding and live our lives out loud, until we claim our beautiful sexuality as just that, being gay will continue to be tabloid material. In a world that has seen every sleazy, ludicrous event and every "shock and awe" variation on violence, rumors or proof that any public figure—a politician, or a movie star, or a TV personality or member of a royal family is gay, *still* qualifies as tantalizing, sensational news, full of potential for its "dirty-sex" marketability. If we don't learn to *embrace our sexuality* as healthy, life-force energy that nurtures and feeds our passion for all kinds of gifts to the world, if we don't stop denying and repressing it, then the entire, intricate chain of human evolution may at some point come grinding to a halt. This is my theory on sexuality.

Love Makes a Family

... is a statewide coalition of organizations and individuals working to expand Connecticut's marriage laws to include same-sex couples. In Connecticut, same-sex couples are currently denied over 588 benefits, protections and responsibilities that come with civil marriage.

In the early stages of her journey to wholeness Pat moved into my house in a beautiful little town in Connecticut, and seemed to think she would simply hide out there, wallowing in self-loathing and lethargy. Most of her family wouldn't see her, she had lost her job and her church community, and no one in my town knew who she was. Our love for each other may well have been all that kept her alive. This was the state of things the day my daughters met a number of handsome young Venezuelan naval officers who came into port nearby as part of a goodwill tour hosted by their father. They wanted to bring their friends home to see where they lived, introduce them to us, and show them our part of New England. "Don't let them come!" said Pat. "They'll think we're gay!"

"We are gay," I reminded her.

Those were the early days, the fragile and uncertain days before we began to live our lives as a couple with conviction and purpose.

Babies and young children will accept anything if it is all they've known. The grandchildren loved us unconditionally. What amazed us was the teenagers—my children and their friends. After the initial fear (given my track record) that my union with Pat would be one more lousy relationship they would have to endure, my daughters behaved as if she and I had raised them all their lives. Not only was this *not* another lousy relationship, but suddenly, they had two mothers! Two mothers is a wonderful thing, it turns out, when you're having your wisdom teeth removed or when you're taken to the hospital by ambulance because you fell off your horse and they think you've broken your neck, or when you're having a nervous breakdown first semester of graduate school. My kids became so attached to Pat that one of them said to her in my presence: "Your children don't know what they're missing. I would have *killed* to have a mother like you!" Then she looked at me with "Ooops" written all over her face and tried unsuccessfully to remove her foot from her mouth.

The morning routine on the occasions when both of my children are home still goes like this: as we try to sleep as far past 7:00 am as possible, these two young adults come into the room at the crack of dawn to jump on us in bed saying, "Get up, get up— it's morning!" They tickle and bounce and invite all the animals up onto the bed to join them until we give in. You would think that at our ages we would be spared this unspeakable behavior, but not a chance.

From the outset, our house seemed to become an anchor for the "lost" teenagers (as I called them) who came to visit. They were bright, creative, beautiful children chronically trying to escape some form of trauma at home. One teen had been raised in a foster home and loved to cook— he was in charge of meals when he came; one flew across the country to spend the summer with us because her stepfather was sexually abusing her. She found in our house a place to work through migraine headaches and hypochondria. Another had never been read to as a child and would curl up next to us on the couch, wide-eyed like a four-year-old, and we would read to him out loud.

We had birthday parties and "coming of age" ceremonies as they turned 18 or 21; we would celebrate New Year's Eve together with the yearly ritual of writing down all that they wanted to let go of from the past year on a little piece of paper, sharing their thoughts out loud if they wanted, then throwing the piece of paper into the fire as a symbol of release. They always spoke, even the timid ones, and their words held wisdom far beyond their years.

Why did my children adjust so quickly to my new relationship, as wary as they were? Why did the others come? What was it that drew them to spend time with us? There's no plausible explanation but that they felt the love that makes us a family, the deep respect we hold for one another, and the lack of conflict or tension. Instead of judging, or holding back because we're "different," these kids simply felt and came toward the love.

One of my daughters had a college boyfriend who was very tall, and very shy. With him we played cards, because playing cards was where he came alive. Unlike the others, he did not come from a troubled home. His family was extremely stable, but they weren't a "physical" family, as my daughter put it. "They never touch, or hug each other hello or good-bye," she told us. "Around here, you can't leave the room without a hug and a kiss!" One night Pat and I were cleaning up the kitchen before bed when this very tall, very shy boy came to the doorway in his pajamas and socks and stood quietly at the threshold.

"Hi Jeff," we said, "What do you need?"

"I came for my good-night kiss," he said very softly.

Will You Marry Us?

January 21, 2001

Dear Bishop, Pat wrote:

Karen and I have been together in a loving, committed relationship for almost three years, and have decided to honor and celebrate our commitment with a holy union ceremony.

We have clergy friends from several denominations who will be with us that day as an integral part of the ceremony. They have, in fact, been eagerly awaiting this event. It is important to me that an Episcopal priest or Bishop bless our holy union as well; I am writing this letter to give you the 'right of first refusal' by asking if you would do us the honor either of blessing our union, or agreeing to be present as a witness.

I do, of course, fully understand the implications of this request, and the conflict it may present for you on many levels. (I was heartened to hear that Bishop Larry Mace of Arkansas is allowing the priests in his diocese to perform holy union ceremonies for same-sex couples, and I pray that Connecticut is not far behind).

The last time you met with the 'openly-gay clergy group' you asked this question about same-sex committed relationships: 'Are they the same as marriage?' I wish I had told you then what I will relate to you now:

Karen's daughter has a college friend who came to visit for a few days this summer. We wondered if he would feel awkward with us because we are a gay couple; he comes from a tiny town in Maine where life is conservative, and most of the people in town, by his own description, are related to one another.

On the contrary, this boy seemed to feel right at home and easily became a part of the household, treating us both as Lesley's parents, which is how she refers to us. One morning Lesley had to go across the street early to help at the farm where she boards her horse, and she left her guest asleep in his room until she came back. He woke up just as Karen and I were having coffee and joined us at the breakfast table, where we talked with him for quite a while.

Weeks later, Lesley told us what her friend had said about the visit: "When I sat with your Mom and Pat at the breakfast table," he told her, "I watched how they talked together, and how they interacted. I don't care what the law says—they're a married couple!"

This young man, who may never have met or sat with another openly-gay couple in his life and would therefore have no reason to see our union as "natural" or "right," saw our relationship for exactly what it is. As did Pat's seven-year-old grandson when he said to her one day, "Is it a real marriage, Nana? It feels real to me!"

I hope that you, too, can see us for who we are, and officially honor our relationship for what it is.

Yours in Christ,

February 26, 2001
Dear Pat, the Bishop wrote:

Your letter of January 21st raises many questions, which I have wanted to take time to ponder and commit to prayer. At this point in the diocese, the long-standing policy, which does not sanction the blessing of same-sex, committed relationships by our diocesan clergy, remains in effect . . . It would *be inconsistent with the policy that is in place for me to preside at a blessing of your relationship with Karen . . .*

Holy Union

Let them love each other openly and without fear,
A joyful sign of new creation in justice, love, and peace,
Bless them so that they may flourish together
And rejoice in their friends.
Grant them the goods that endure
And bring them to everlasting joy.
Create for them a life inhabited by
Divine love And a home in which no one is a stranger.
Defend them from every danger,
And lead them into all peace. Amen.

—From the clergy blessing at the Holy Union of Pat and Karen, June 2,
2001

The ushers said it was easy to spot the heterosexuals as they approached. To a person, they looked around nervously, clutched their opposite-gender partner, and slowed down as they got to the door as if not sure what would become of them if they entered. One had asked in advance if we were both going to wear white wedding gowns, because if we were, it might be "too much" for her husband to bear and she wasn't sure she could convince him to come. Some of them, when handed the bulletin, stood motionless at the threshold: to take a seat inside might commit them to something beyond their ability to cope. One poor man stood helplessly adrift, announcing loudly (to protect against gay advances, no doubt): *"I've lost my wife. She was just here, and now I can't find her!"*

These heterosexual people came to the ceremony because they are our friends and they love us, and so—despite their anxiety—they joined our gay sisters and brothers, and our families, and colleagues from all walks of life and religious traditions in a building that was filled to capacity on United Church of Christ property. We couldn't use the majestic church building right next door because the minister—already out on a limb—was afraid it would put the congregation over the edge. But he let us fill the church both before and after the ceremony with musicians rehearsing, people changing clothes, cooks preparing food, and drummers entertaining guests until the buffet was set and the dinner served.

We made a chapel of the little building next to the church. Every seat in the room was taken. The altar hosted more purple candles than most people see in a lifetime, and by the time the flute and piano began the prelude and the candles were lit one by one and the room was "smudged" with sage to create sacred space and the flowers were brought down the aisle and the presiding clergy began to "process," you could feel the magic in the room.

From the back a soloist sang *"Breath of God"* with a voice like an angel, and nobody moved. Pat and I came through the doorway together, then separated to walk to opposite corners of the room. We waited for the question that came from the altar: *"Patricia Gallagher, why are you here?"* And then: *"Karen Hunter, why are you here?"*

We spoke out loud of our love, our challenges, and our desire to pave the way for those who would follow. This was our chance to publicly address the people courageous enough to take the journey with us; this was a day that would change all of our lives forever. It was not to be taken lightly or unadvisedly. When we finished speaking the drummers began to play, slowly and rhythmically, then increasing in power, as Pat and I came together and walked down the aisle with some of our children at our sides.

The sermon "brought down the house" and banished separation with its intensity, humor, and honesty as we became one people united in sacred space for the purpose of spreading love. We were old and young, partnered and single, strong of body and physically handicapped, religious and non-religious, gay and straight, fat and thin, tall and short, women and men. Embraced within this spectrum as broad as a rainbow we made our commitment:

In the mystery of Divine love,
You have been given to me.
I take you, the joy of my heart and soul,
To be mine before God and humanity.
I promise to stand with you in adversity;
To support you in honest self-expression;
To hold you gently when you are feeling overwhelmed.
I promise to listen to your voice and to hear your heart;
To respect your sorrow and your joy;
To be a source of strength, comfort, and happiness.
I promise to love, honor, and cherish you until the end of
our time.

Four clergy from four denominations, including an Episcopal priest, performed the Sacrament of Holy Eucharist and invited everyone to come forward:

This is an open communion. We are keenly aware that at
this table all barriers are mute, all distinctions are neu-
tral, all grievances are pointless, for the invitation of the
Host is clear . . . all are welcome at the banquet feast!

Two choral groups, female and male, stood together during communion to sing *"Dona Nobis Pacem"* in harmony and round, over and over and over. *Give us peace, give us peace, give us peace.*

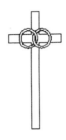

It's Like Being with a Celebrity

When Pat was removed as priest-in-charge of her parish upon coming out, one family who had been in the parish for over fifty years extracted a promise from the bishop that she be allowed to come back to the church as the celebrant when their daughters were ready to marry. Five years went by before the bishop was called upon to grant his promise, but eventually a wedding was planned.

The bride asked if I would do a reading; I told her it would be an honor. On rehearsal night she asked if I could also take care of a "few" other items on the list: hand out programs at the beginning of the service and bubble-blowing material for people to blow at the end, line up the bridesmaids for the processional and be sure each one knew when to start down the aisle, hold back the flower girl until the "runner" had been run from the altar so the rose petals could be scattered upon it, hand the two young ring bearers their ring pillows and hold them still for the line-up, signal the priest when the bridesmaids were ready so she could signal the harpist to begin the processional, and, above all, be sure that the ushers got the blue buttoniers, the ring bearers got the small white and the groom the large white flowers, and the grandmother of the bride, the corsage with carnations. I didn't know who most of these people *were*, but that didn't seem to be an issue. Finally I was to close the doors to the church so the bride and her parents could approach the entrance from outside without being seen by the congregation or the groom. Once they were in place behind closed doors and the music had changed accordingly, the doors were to be opened, and the rest would be written in stone until death did them part.

The groom had six brothers and a couple of sisters, and the bride had a few people to add to the wedding party. I have never seen as many ushers in a wedding that wasn't held in Westminster Abby. Not only did I have to nab them as they wandered at loose ends around the church an hour before the service, I had to pin their flowers onto them. No men, and very few women, can ever do this successfully on their own. This was an Italian wedding. The ushers were big, beefy, macho young men. Fumbling with flowers and pins at their lapels brought me closer to that much masculinity than I had been in many years. They all seemed so tall—towering patiently over me as I tried not to stab while making light conversation to ease the awkwardness. The exception to the Italian, but not the tall, rule was a gorgeous blond man who had such height on him that the ring bearer said, "Boy are you tall!"

"How tall are you?" I asked, hoping he wouldn't notice that his buttonier might end up somewhere around his navel unless I got a stool.

"Six/six," he said.

"I once had a husband who was six/six," I said with a laugh, in an unconscious attempt to make him think I was your basic heterosexual woman.

"So did I!" he said.

Our eyes met.

"Bravo!" was what I thought—for putting it right out there in casual conversation; he already knew who I was and I felt ashamed for trying to hide it.

"Good for you," was what I said. "Good for you."

The reception was traditional and elegant with phenomenal food and service and a magnificent setting along the Connecticut River. The DJ was energetic with a genuine sense of humor—a refreshing change from the usual obnoxious and obscene—and the music was the kind that had a real tune! When dinner was over and the cake had been cut, the dancing began. We sat with our coffee, listened and watched, and talked with the bride's family and friends until the DJ cleared the dance floor and asked that all married couples come to the floor. "All couples please come forward," he announced several times. Pat and I froze, like deer in the headlights. "We're a couple," I said, "We have to go." The dance floor was filled with conservative "old-school" couples, an amazing number of whom had been married more than fifty years. We found a place near people we knew and the music started for a long, slow dance. I held my female partner, and she held me, and we sang the words to each other as we moved, trying not to look around, trying not to notice if we were being noticed, trying not to care. In that large group of heterosexual people gathered to celebrate marital love, we felt completely alone and completely exposed. My knees began to shake. "This takes a lot of guts," Pat whispered in my ear.

We had no choice. If for no one else, we had to get up and dance for that beautiful blond usher who was watching every move we made; we had to make it normal by simply making it normal; we had to dance together for people to see what it looks like; we had to be who we are— even there—because that's what we have committed to do. Several lifetimes passed during that dance, but eventually the music stopped and we could make our way back to our seats. I walked with lowered eyes; I couldn't bear to look at the room—until I heard noise at the table next to ours and saw a cousin of the bride clapping loudly with her hands held over her head for all to see. "That was great!" she said. "I wanted my mother to see that." I looked up and smiled, exhaling for the first time in twenty minutes, as the muscles beneath my shoulder blades began to relax.

Extricating ourselves from weddings and funerals is always a lengthy process because everyone wants to talk to the priest. I followed Pat around the room, carrying the raincoats and umbrellas that had gotten us through the pouring rain from the church to the car and from the car to the reception hall. A large backpack over my shoulder held everything we would need for the day: a bible, extra shoes, the sermon, a camera, a folder full of notes, a hairbrush, and a cell phone. In fact, I make the perfect support person—efficient, tireless, and uncomplaining—and as I stood to the side of a group of people with whom Pat was entangled, a woman at the next table who had been watching me grabbed my arm and said, "It's like being with a celebrity!"

"Very much so!" I agreed.

"It takes a special kind of person to play that role," she said. "You two must have a wonderful relationship!"

What she meant, expressed through her generosity of words and compassionate heart, was: "I see who you are; it's OK to be gay." Hers was the third validation in a matter of hours on that rainy day when the best I had hoped for was to survive unscathed. Gratitude seeped into my pores, softened my heart and dissolved my body armor, for if a high-profile lesbian couple which happens to include the *priest* can be seen and honored at a traditional, heterosexual, wedding then the world *is* changing. Slowly but surely, we are changing the world.

Spanish Class

My feisty, strong-willed, second daughter spent the formative years of her childhood in Central America, where—unlike her older sister—she refused to learn to speak Spanish. "I don't *want* to speak Spanish," she would announce with all the emphasis of a three-year-old coming into a sense of her own power, thereby creating a great opportunity lost.

Lesley started talking about the Peace Corps in high school and, by college, was choosing courses with State Department service in mind. People who serve in either organization need at least a second language, so as a college junior, she signed up for beginner's Spanish.

For reasons that would have seemed like a joke when Lesley was three, Spanish class became a challenge right from the start. It wasn't about conjugating the verbs or rolling the "r's," or trying to decipher the teacher's accent and teaching style. It was the "family tree" assignment. Writing down one's family tree is an excellent way to practice descriptive and relational nouns, and Lesley dutifully put her genealogy to paper. She surprised herself by hesitating at the step-parents. Should she name her gay grandfather's male partner? Her mother's female partner? This was, remember, the second week of class. Her creative solution was to list blood relations, and draw a "happy face" where step-people could have been named, including her father's wife and her grandmother's husband so it was an across-the-board omission. Afterward, she found herself embarrassed by her lack of honesty, for as she said, "I have an awesome family; why should I have to hide any of them?" She resolved to make it up at another time.

As karma would have it, the opportunity presented itself the following week when the Spanish class assignment was to bring in a family *photograph* and stand at the front of the class to name and describe each person in the picture. Supported by her resolve to speak with conviction and without embarrassment, Lesley took the fateful photograph from her high school graduation to class—the one with all of us standing shoulder to shoulder squinting into the sun trying to pretend we were like any other family.

Lesley is afraid of almost nothing. She will ride a horse that no one else can ride, make a perfect swan dive off the side of a cliff into an icy pool of water in a remote area of a third-world country, scale the face of a mountain in the middle of the night in the pouring rain with a sixty-pound pack on her back to reach a campsite, fly in anything with wings, and—from the frantic report I got the summer she spent with her grandfather in the Berkshires—play a game of "chicken" with a friend by jumping off the train trestle into the rapids of the Deerfield River thirty feet below. Speaking in public, however, reduces her to sheer panic. She's not alone: most people fear speaking in public more than they fear having cancer, a fact which becomes the most neutral of points when your body is shaking from head to toe, your teeth are rattling in your head, and you can't breathe as you walk to the front of the class clutching your family photo in sweaty hands. Of all the opportunities to wrestle with a phobia of public speaking, this particular class assignment probably wasn't the place to start. The idea is to be *comfortable* with your material! I'm sure the words "where do I begin?" crossed what was left of Lesley's ability to think as she took the obvious tact of naming people from left to right:

"My step-mother (madrasta) is in the chaqueta blanca (white jacket). She is 'generosa.' Her husband in the uniform is my father Felipe; el es muy alto (he is very tall). Al lado de mi padre es mi hermana en el vestido negra (to the side of my father is my sister in the black dress); ella es muy delgado y muy bonita (she is very thin and very beautiful).

"Mi mama en la chaqueta violetta es muy intelligente (my mother in the purple jacket is very intelligent). Se llama Karen. Her name is Karen. Su esposa, mi madrasta (her wife, my step-mother), es un priest Episcopal . . ."

With these words Lesley discovered for herself the fastest way to bring a room full of people to a standstill. Her classmates became a frozen mass of bodies—Sympathetic? Unsympathetic? Curious? Horrified?—she didn't know, and the teacher looked up from her notes so fast that she could have been treated for whiplash. The silence was deafening. Lesley stood there for a minute listening to her body shake, then concluded her presentation by saying: "There is a lot of tension in this picture!" and took her seat.

She laughed on the phone when she called to say, "You're 'out' at college, Mom!" and told me the story. We laughed together, but I wanted to cry for what she had gone through, for my heart was saying, "I'm so sorry Lesley, I'm so sorry." The image of her standing alone and exposed at the front of the class because she refused to hide is the image of every one of us who risks exposure by standing up and refusing to hide. And it rarely gets any easier. At best, we can only cheer each other on and hope that the rest of the world catches up while we're alive to enjoy it,

You go, girl!

At the end of that academic year, Lesley enrolled in an intensive French course in preparation for two months of visiting Peace Corps villages in the French-speaking Central African country of Gabon. If she had thought about it, she might have foreseen, and therefore prepared herself, for the brutal fact that one of the first assignments would be, again,"the family tree."

This is Christianity

What's it like, being a gay vicar? Well, I prepare a sermon and a Sunday service every week. People tell me their troubles and their joys. They comment on the music, complain about the lights, stay for coffee and introduce me to the people they have brought along. I visit my key lay people, have various meetings with them through the week, and meet regularly with clergy colleagues—Protestant, Catholic and Anglican. There are usually at least a dozen people involved in making the Sunday service happen: musicians, readers, intercessors. We all work together as a team.

And then every so often a rock comes hurtling through the air completely unexpectedly—You forget. That's the thing. You forget that it's an issue—it's just your ordinary life.

—Anonymous gay vicar, northern England, *The Guardian*,

The week was like any other in a small industrial city forty-five minutes from our home. Pat had been at her church just a year. Everyone knew she was gay, and everyone knew she was living in a committed relationship with a woman. She had told the Search Committee and the Vestry during the interview before she was hired, and when I attended Sunday services she always introduced me as her partner. The bishop had done the same at her "installation" ceremony. For a year everything had been going amazingly well within this very conservative congregation. Only one family had left because of the "homosexual issue," and their departure was more than offset by the increasing number of people who came to church every week as word spread about the new priest.

Every church has its core group of dedicated parishioners and hard workers—the people who help the priest keep the church alive. Karl and his family were among them. They ran a small business in town and donated generously to church events and fund-raisers; both husband and wife were on committees that comprised the business arm of the church, and Karl took pride in the landscaping work that kept the church grounds looking good. From the beginning, while most of the congregation was tentative and would formally shake hands with the new priest at the end of the service, Karl would give Pat a hug and a kiss on the cheek as he went out the door. She thought he was a beautiful man; she valued their relationship and their common desire to see the church grow to its potential.

Just as she would any other week, she made a phone call one day to Karl with a question about the men's group. *I was going to call you,* he said, *to tell you that I'm leaving the church. I have to tell you that I don't believe in women's ordination; it's not in the Bible.*

Pat was speechless.

And that other thing.

What other thing? she asked.

That other thing that you are.

You mean that I'm homosexual?

The Bible says that it's wrong and that it's a sin. I've been talking to a Jehovah's Witness and other Christians. We talk about the Bible all the time; it's an abomination. The devil is in our church.

Through her shock, Pat tried to answer, but she quickly realized that there was no talking to him. His pronouncement was rigid and final. What had *happened*? There was that rock hurtling unexpectedly through the air. "Blind-sided," she told me. "I felt completely blind-sided. This doesn't make sense. How could I have prepared myself for this? How could *this* be Christianity?

May We Pray With You?

The Episcopal Diocese was beginning to get a little nervous over the homosexual issue. The "evangelicals" were vocal and insistent that "active" homosexuality or "practicing homosexuals" not be tolerated among Episcopal clergy, yet openly gay clergy were coming out of seminary, coming out in general, taking parishes, performing holy unions, and living with their partners in church rectories. Before this book was finished, an openly-gay priest had been elected bishop of New Hampshire. Things were clearly getting out of hand.

Many months before that happened, the Bishop of the Diocese of Connecticut organized a meeting for conservative and liberal clergy to discuss this issue, and Pat was asked to attend. The meeting was taken seriously enough to enlist the help of two facilitators from Plowshare Peace and Justice Center, an organization committed to the creation of a just world peace that has a component called Respect for Diversity. *We seek to encourage creative and compassionate interaction among genders, races, classes and religions within our community and worldwide based on justice and mutual respect,* is their stated purpose.[29]

Clergy from opposite sides of the "does God say it's OK to be gay" line assembled and sat in seats placed in a large circle, to receive instructions on how the day would proceed (no name-calling or physical violence, etc), and to take a minute or two to introduce themselves before moving to smaller groups for discussion on passages from scripture. Pat was one of two women in the room, and the only "out" priest.

"It's hard enough, as a woman, to sit in a room with the "old boy network,'" she explained, "but having to talk about being openly gay as well was almost unbearable. I knew I was in the minority; I knew how strongly many of the others stood against the gay 'issue' because they were vocal about it. I could feel tension, discomfort, and disdain infecting the air around me as I spoke. How would we ever hear one another? How would anything ever change? Every conservative person in the room had a deeply-held position to cling to, and each of us thought the other was unreasonable, irrational, or at the very least uninformed. A number of supportive clergy were present, but all they could do was be supportive; I was the one—the only one—who talked about being gay. The conservative clergy directed their anger at me and I could feel it. The talk was polite enough, but talk couldn't mask the hostility seeping from their pores. As incomprehensible as it may seem for a gathering of clergy, the point of the meeting was to learn to love one another as human beings. In the eyes of the conservatives, however, I ranked first and foremost as an 'abomination.' Their hearts were closed and locked, as far as I could tell."

She remembered a passage from an article written by Trinity College chaplain Steven Charleston after the death of Matthew Shepard: *Silence killed Matthew Shepard. The silence of Christians who know that our scriptures on homosexuality are few and murky in interpretation and are far outweighed by the words of a savior whose only comment on human relationships was to call us to never judge but only to love . . . we are men and women surrounded by the silence of our own fear: Our fear of those who are different. Our fear of being identified with the scapegoat. Our fear of taking an unpopular position for the sake of those who can not stand alone. Our fear of social and religious change.*[30]

A journal entry she had made while reading Pierre Wolffe's book *Is God Deaf?* came to mind: *I will lead her into the dessert and speak to her heart (Hosea 2: 16),* the chapter began. *Reading scripture sends me into a fury these days,* she wrote. *Not because of the exclusivity of the writing or the words of oppression, which are a reflection of their time, but because the Church refuses to endorse a change in the way we see things; it refuses to open up the canons for re-writing 2,000 years later, now that we are a different people at a different stage of evolution. Is God Deaf? I believe not. Are we deaf? Absolutely!*

I face a captivity of ignorance, her journal-entry continued, *an imprisonment of hurt, a torture of unbearable fundamental principles taken from a book passed down through generations to impose the sins of many and allow for slavery, wars, and oppression of all kinds. Sometimes I feel we should rip it up and start all over—or at the very least, learn from it, take ourselves to a new level and write more to leave for the next generation.*

All this was swirling in her heart as she spoke about her path, and her pain. She spoke openly to the group about who she is, about her long heterosexual marriage and painful divorce, about coming out, about living with her partner and trying to make her way in the world and in the church. She asked only that no one insult her by suggesting that she could change if she really wanted to, for, she explained, she had spent her entire life trying to "change." As she spoke from her heart and exposed her vulnerability, her defenses melted and her anger disappeared. No one interrupted; no one attacked.

The agenda turned to the passages from scripture selected for discussion. They were neutral passages—nothing from Genesis, Leviticus, or Romans; nothing from Corinthians, or Timothy. Nothing that could be construed as support for, or condemnation of, homosexuality. Her mind has now gone blank on what they discussed. What she does remember is that they got to know each other as human beings. As they talked quietly about what the scripture passages meant to them from a personal point of view, the tension in the room began to ease.

The Ploughshares facilitator gave the ending prayer and the day came to a close. In the milling about before people left, a priest approached Pat, taking her by surprise. "Could I talk to you for a minute?" he asked. She turned to see who he was and found herself looking into the face of a man from the "conservative," "anti-gay" side of the room. "I hope I didn't insult you and your partner in anything that I said," he told her. "I didn't mean it personally." Before she could reply, another "anti-gay" priest joined them, and then another. The first one said, "Would it be OK if I prayed with you?" Pat hesitated. She was afraid. Was he going to try to "save" her? Would he offer a fundamentalist prayer about hating the sin but loving the sinner? Would she be trapped, holding hands, head bowed in prayer with priests who thought she was perverted and sending a supplication to God that she be allowed to correct her ways through God's mercy and grace?

Her intuition, which has never led her astray, told her to go ahead, and she agreed. A calmness came over her body. She and these men who had so frightened her put their arms around one another and formed a huddle. One priest spoke. Transcending their differences, he prayed for her journey, he prayed for her partner, he prayed for our life together. Then they hugged with respect for one another as valuable, vulnerable human beings, and went their separate ways. Deaf, perhaps, no more.

The bishop never called this group together again; the softening that had occurred went un-addressed and therefore unsupported, and the huge potential for change melted quietly into the woodwork.

Pride

*Enflame our entire community, dear God, and be the force
that drives us to honesty, clarity, commitment, and truth.
Clear our ears so that together, we may hear your call to
unite. Be with us as we strive to create a world that is
safe for closet doors to open everywhere, and for the spir-
ited and the lovely to emerge.*
Lord, with your love,
Receive our prayer.

—Kelly Turney, Editor, *Shaping Sanctuary*

D*ear Bishop,* Pat wrote:

*Twelve members of the Sanctuary community marched yester-
day in the Gay Pride Hartford parade behind our banner. Among
us were a UCC minister, a Yale Divinity School seminarian, a
former Methodist minister, and an ex-US Marine and his wife, a
Presbyterian minister. Our place in line was in front of several of
the local Open and Affirming Congregational churches and Dignity of the Roman Catholic Church.*

*As we came around the corner approaching Christ Cathedral
in downtown Hartford, I pointed out to our group that we were
coming upon the Episcopal Cathedral, and there was a somber
silence as we all looked up at its imposing form. It is hard to
describe what happens emotionally when marching for gay pride
in front of a cathedral with a group of people deeply wounded
and long oppressed by the Church. It felt like facing the embodiment of the oppressor; like entering a long shadow that would
block the sun and send a shiver down our spines.*

Suddenly, we saw the large banner stretched across the structure's entrance:

A gasp, and then a huge cheer, went up among us. Those simple words on that banner were like a blast of light and warmth that honored, affirmed, supported, and included us. The greatest sense of pride for me that day came from seeing that message on "my" church. This is to acknowledge, with great appreciation, the bishops' part in that. May peace and understanding fill your days.

You Are Feeding My People

Although God loves everyone, he does not condone sinful behavior . . . the Bible equates homosexuality with perversity and as Christians we cannot interpret God's word to suit modern life-styles . . . It is devilish and satanic. It comes directly from the pit of hell. It is an idea sponsored by Satan himself and being executed by his followers and adherents who have infiltrated the church.

—Louis Green, African Christian Democratic Party in South Africa

Dear Pat,

With peace, grace and love of Christ, I greet you from Liberia. Though St. Augustine's Episcopal Church has expressed thanks and appreciation to you, the vestry, and the congregation of Christ Episcopal Church for the second round of assistance in the amount of $840, I as priest, whose ministry you are tremendously promoting in these troubled times of my congregation, add my voice to theirs in thanking you.

Your gifts to the church make the church more relevant to its members and some community members. It restored the lost hope of my people. You are feeding my people at the time food cannot be found, and often if found, the price is unaffordable. Pat, I take to heart your demonstrated love, care, and concern for my ministry and my people. Your kindness has brought you and me closer though we are living miles of miles away from each other. It made your heart, mind, and feelings known to me though we have never met.

Pat, your gesture in the life of St. Augustine's Episcopal Church at this particular time can be compared to the manna

from heaven to the Children of Israel.

It should not be only at misfortune one must ask 'why me.' Even in His undeserved blessing one should be able to ask, 'why me?' Why must your kindness rain on me? God, the possessor of all answers said 'it is more blessed to give than to receive.'

May God bless you and your family, and promote your ministry.

Yours in Christ,

Rev. Father Edward Gbe

St. Augustine Episcopal Church, Kakata, Margibi County, Post Office Box 0277, Manrovia, Liberia, (011) 37747-522753

Homosexuality and the Bible

*To use the Bible like an infallible law book that needs no
interpretation is an absurd position to hold, but it only
really matters when it prompts people to persecute their
neighbors, as has been the case with the Church's treatment of homosexuals.*

—Richard Holloway,*Love and Doubts*

Dear Dr. Laura,

*Thank you for doing so much to educate people regarding God's
law. I have learned a great deal from you, and I try to share that
knowledge with as many people as I can. When someone tries to
defend the homosexual life-style, I simply remind him or her that
Leviticus 18: 22 clearly states it to be an abomination. End of
debate. I do need some advice from you, however, regarding some
of the specific laws and how to best follow them.*

*When I burn a bull on the altar as a sacrifice, I know it cre-
ates a pleasing odor for the Lord (Lev. 1:9). The problem is my
neighbors. They claim the odor is not pleasing to them. How
should I deal with this?*

*I would like to sell my daughter into slavery, as it suggests in
Exodus 21:7. In this day and age, what do you think would be a
fair price for her?*

*I know that I am allowed no contact with a woman while she
is in her period of menstrual uncleanliness (Lev. 15:19-24). The
problem is, how do I tell? I have tried asking, but most women
take offense.*

*Lev. 25:44 states that I may buy slaves from the nations that
are around us. A friend of mine claims that this applies to Mexi-*

cans but not Canadians. Can you clarify?

I have a neighbor who insists on working on the Sabbath. Exodus 35:2 clearly states he should be put to death. Am I morally obligated to kill him myself?

A friend of mine feels that even though eating shellfish is an abomination (Lev. 10:10), it is a lesser abomination than homosexuality. I don't agree. Can you settle this?

Lev. 20:20 states that I may not approach the altar of God if I have a defect in my sight. I have to admit that I wear reading glasses. Does my vision have to be 20/20, or is there some wiggle room here?

I know you have studied these things extensively, so I am confident you can help. Thank you again for reminding us that God's word is eternal and unchanging.

A fan (This was posted on the Internet and widely circulated by email).

Dr. Laura is an author and popular radio personality with a call-in talk show.

―――――――

Many authors have addressed, and put to rest, the issue of "homosexuality and the bible." Marilyn Bennett Alexander and James Preston, in their book *We Were Baptized Too*, do so particularly concisely:

"Unfortunately, the Bible is often used within and without the Church as a selective weapon of oppression rather than as a tool for liberation . . .The word homosexual was not even in the English language until 1897, and it first appeared in a biblical translation in 1952 with the release of the Revised Standard Version. The original biblical languages of Hebrew and Greek have no word for homosexuality, let alone specific vocabulary to connote any particular understanding of sexuality, gender identity, or sexual orientation.

Genesis 19 and Judges 19 are stories of gang rape and protection of male visitors. They address violence toward and subjugation of men. They are not about men loving men; they are about men forcing other men into humiliating submission (the same low status of women). 'Their intent was homosexual rape, which (precisely like its heterosexual counterpart) is the dehumanization of one human being by another' . . . and to quote scholar Peter Gomes, 'To suggest that Sodom and Gomorrah is about homosexual sex is an analysis of about as much worth as suggesting that the story of Jonah and the whale is a treatise on fishing.'

Leviticus 18:22 and 20:13 are verses that focus on men and their role within a patriarchal society. They have nothing to do with gay/lesbian love; in fact, lesbian sex is not even prohibited . . . For readers bent on culling from the Bible a blanket condemnation of 'homosexuality' this omission (the prohibition of lesbian sex) is an embarrassment.

First Corinthians 6:9-11 and 1 Timothy 1:10 do not address homosexuality, but focus on idolatrous activity. The problem with both passages is the ambiguity of the translations of two important words: *arsenokoites* and *malakos*. The writers of these passages were concerned with the matter of male prostitution and pederasty (adult men having sex with boys), not with mutual, loving relationships between two adult men.

Romans 1:26-27 is certainly the most specific text about same-gender sex. It is also the only scriptural passage that mentions sex between women. Yet it must be noted that Paul had no understanding of modern sexual identity, of sexual orientation, or of the possibility of same-gender covenantal love relationships . . . Homoerotic acts were considered evil in a Hellenistic culture because they were thought to be motivated by lust, did not promote procreation, and abandoned the traditional gender roles of a patriarchal society."[31]

"What saddens me most in this whole raucous debate," says theologian Walter Wink in his booklet *Homosexuality and the Bible*, "is how sub-Christian most of it has been. It is characteristic of our time that the issues most difficult to assess, and which have generated the greatest degree of animosity, are issues on which the Bible can be interpreted as supporting either side. I am referring to abortion and homosexuality . . . We in the church need to get our priorities straight. We have not reached a consensus about who is right on the issue of homosexuality. But what is clear, utterly clear, is that we are commanded to love one another."[32]

The Archbishop of Canterbury

Therefore having weighed and considered the matter with the assistance of the learned in law, We do by virtue of the authority vested in Us confirm the Election of the Most Reverend Rowan Douglas Williams to the See of Canterbury.

—Final Declaration of the Commissioners, Episcopal News Service

Archbishop Rowan will be warmly received as a man of deep spiritual resources who cares intensely for the poor, oppressed and the marginalized in society. I look forward to working with him.

—The Rev. Canon John L. Peterson, Secretary General of the Anglican Communion

The Queen of England sets in motion the apparatus for appointing a new archbishop of the "Anglican Communion" by accepting the resignation of the previous archbishop. The appointment process then works its way through an amazing trajectory which involves the "Vicar-General" and the "Court of Arches" and eventually a final decision by the Prime Minister of England and election by the Diocese of Canterbury.

We had such hope. "As a supporter of women priests and homosexuals, Dr. Williams was felt to have the charisma and the catholicity necessary to lead the Church of England into the 21st century," said *The Times of London*.[33] Williams has "a rare combination of un-pious personal holiness with an impressive theological intelligence which does not lose touch with the reality of everyday life. More than that, he has a personal warmth which enables him to deal easily with people of all backgrounds," observed *The Independent*. Distinguished as the only person to have been Professor of Divinity at both Oxford and Cambridge Universities, Rowan Williams is also the first Welshman in at least a *thousand years* to assume the post of Archbishop of Canterbury and the first to be selected from *outside the Church of England* since the Reformation (He's an "outsider!"). He has written extensively on human sexuality and in support of the full inclusion of homosexuals in the life of the Church, and he is in contact with leaders of a variety of gay and lesbian groups (He's a liberal!). If the Queen dies, the Archbishop of Canterbury is next in line to be Head of State after the immediate royal family. (He's in a position of power!) We had such hope.

Rowan Williams, known to be liberal, out-spoken, highly intellectual, and already at odds with conservative Anglicans, was "enthroned" as Archbishop of Canterbury on February 27th, 2003, and the riot began. Before this occasion, the British press had reported: "Traditionalists opposed to the views of the Archbishop of Canterbury, Dr. Rowan Williams, on issues such as gay sex are to protest outside his enthronement. Some will be wearing black armbands when Dr. Williams is enthroned on Thursday in a ceremony attended by Christian leaders at Canterbury Cathedral."[34] *The Atlanta Journal and Constitution* had this to say: "Williams' personal sympathies toward inclusion of homosexuals in the church run counter to the beliefs of most of those who oversee the quickly growing churches in places such as Asia, Africa, and South America. Many Anglican archbishops in Africa, for example, where more than half the world's Anglicans reside, speak of the Western churches' liberal trends as 'satanic.'"[35] *The Daily Telegraph* wrote this: "The Archbishop of Canterbury will try to avert schism in the Church's worldwide war over homosexuality when he attends a summit of Anglican leaders this week. Dr. Rowan Williams and his fellow primates . . . will debate a report which gives warning of 'anarchy and division' if liberal bishops permit homosexual 'marriages . . .'"[36]

Anglicans waited and watched. Gay Anglicans in particular. They didn't have long to wait before the inevitable occurred. Within months of taking office, the archbishop was faced with the appointment of an openly-gay priest as Bishop of Reading (England). The appointee, Jeffrey John, had been in committed relationship with his male partner for 27 years and had no intention of leaving him (although he shared with the world that their relationship was now "celibate"). Jeffrey John is the author of a booklet on gay relationships, *Permanent, Faithful, Stable*, and has urged the church to recognize same-sex unions.

This was a crisis. The African churches, headed by Nigeria, threatened to "split the Church of England" if it proceeded with the consecration of its first gay bishop (*The Guardian*, June 20, 2003) and the Sydney Anglican diocese widened its list of banned clergy to include celibate homosexuals and those who had pre-marital sex but failed to repent (*The Australian*, June 25, 2003). "God could split the church in order to purge it of 'false teachers,'" one hysterical church-goer told *The Reading Evening Post*[37], and the Queen was on record as feeling "deeply concerned" by the escalating rift in the Church of England over the appointment.[38]

"Until now," allowed *The Independent* of London, "Archbishop Williams might be excused his initial hesitations in the face of an overwhelming onslaught of hysteria from the anti-gay lobby. He has tried to buy time, to . . . avoid having to make a choice between his Catholic sense of the importance of sacramental unity and his Protestant instinct for the truth."[39]

Well, time was up, and here was the test of character. If Rowan Williams had been as unshakeable in his support of homosexual rights within the church as he has been in his stance against war, the Anglican Church might have begun to inch its way out of the dark ages. This, however, was not to be. The Archbishop of Canterbury held a six-hour meeting at Lambeth Palace at which Jeffery John was forced to step down as the bishop of Reading. Liberals were furious. Gay rights campaigners protested what they called the "sexual apartheid." The Dean of Southwark said the Anglican Church was presenting an image of "narrowness, bigotry, and prejudice."[40] Finally, Bishop John Shelby Spong summed up the situation with his usual candor: "I have studied the lives of effective leaders for a long time," he wrote. Unfortunately, the Archbishop of Canterbury, Rowan Williams, is not destined to be one of them . . . I had great hopes for his career. He has, however, been a constant disappointment . . . "[41]

So much for the Archbishop of Canterbury!

Homosexuality and the Church

The Church's act of silencing lesbians and gays is not a passive or benevolent act of love.

—James Empereur, *Spiritual Direction and the Gay Person*

I'm not the first gay bishop;
I'm just the first one to be honest about it.

—Bishop Gene Robinson, New Hampshire

In my experience the only difference between a gathering of MCC (gay) clergy and a gathering of Episcopal— or any other— clergy is that with very few exceptions the former are out of the closet and the latter are not. It is well known in gay circles that the church is a bastion of homosexuality, and that if the gay clergy and organists were forced to leave, churches everywhere would collectively close their doors. I remember my father's utter amazement after he came out and moved to Washington, D.C., about the number of gay Catholic priests (and their partners!) to whom he was introduced at his first high-society gay party, and I've heard Bishop John Spong recount that by the time he retired as Bishop of Newark, NJ, 35 of his priests had come out of the closet, and 31 of them had partners. He also spoke of African Bishops who have confided to him that they are gay, despite the statement by African Anglicans that they don't have homosexuals in their church because "homosexuality is a British disease."

The sad fact about the human race is that we fear most that which we do not want to look at within ourselves, or within our institutions. Watching the cumbersome gyrations of the Church as it tries to maneuver around denial of the primacy of homosexuality within its ranks and potentially within its congregations is like watching a dinosaur swat a mosquito, or an elephant dance on a tight-rope. It doesn't compute. It feels schizophrenic. The truth exists in plain view, and there is an entire institution pretending not to see it. Instead, emergency meetings are held with bishops and archbishops and even the Pope. Somber "processing sessions" are convened to try and figure out how to remain "one body in Christ" in the face of (the brave few) openly-homosexual Christians claiming to be children of God too—and, God forbid, asking to have their unions blessed by the Church.

Large conventions of closeted clergy create committees and task forces to "study" the "issue" of homosexuality within the Church, to "seek the mind of Christ" in all things (as if the Church's systemic oppression of homosexuals has anything to do with the mind of Christ), and to discern how to be sensitive to the "opposition" by making sure their voices are heard. Hearing this, one gay priest asked a bishop at a recent meeting in the Connecticut Diocese: "Would we have invited the KKK to talks on racism to be sure *their* voices were heard?" This was the same meeting where one bishop's advice to an audience of openly clergy and their supporters was: "You need to be patient with injustice."

Which begs the question: "Why?"

For me, as an outsider who has never taken the Church as any kind of authority over my life, this situation is a farce of staggering proportions. Can't everyone *see* that the Emperor has no clothes? In Connecticut, I watch speechlessly as grown adults—often known to their congregations as intelligent, competent and even dynamic priests—sit in the presence of "their" bishop, year after year, hoping against hope that if he hears their stories, their questions and their pleas enough times, he will (finally) condescend to take the necessary steps to fully endorse their humanity. When will the Episcopal Church start to celebrate the ordination of Gene Robinson, as if something good and right has happened, instead of defending it as if something bad and wrong has occurred? When will priests be allowed to perform holy unions (and have holy unions to legitimize their own relationships), and when will the church write a liturgy for those ceremonies? ("We've been discussing this for *twenty years* within the church," one gay priest protested. "At this point I'm hoping it will happen in my lifetime."). When will the Diocese endorse—or dare we suggest—*initiate*, something—anything—proactive for gay rights? Education within the parishes? An LGBT ministry (modeled after those that already exist in other Episcopal Dioceses so no wheel would even have to be reinvented)? Workshops? Support groups? Programs for gay youth and their families?

After hours "in dialogue," (a tactic the bishops seem to favor above all else because, while it looks as though they are actually *doing* something, they can be "in dialogue" until the end of time without taking the risk of a leadership decision), the gay clergy and their supporters leave yet another meeting, clinging to the scraps they've been thrown in the form of Christian-coated platitudes (the most appalling platitudes of all), while not one authoritative step, courageous or otherwise, has been promised, or even proposed, to change anything. This, in my experience, is homosexuality and the Church.

Gene Robinson

The Lesbian and Gay Christian Movement is to hold a conference in Manchester next week at which Canon Gene Robinson will speak by live video link-up. . . he had originally planned to attend but has been advised not to travel by the FBI after receiving death threats. He is currently under 24-hour guard.

—GAYFAITHNEWS@ONELIST.com

To fundamentalists in the US, who launched a witch-hunt last week to scupper his ordination, and Africa, threatening to break free from the colonial yolk of Lambeth Palace, disgusted by the West's heathen ways, he has become the anti-Christ. . . .

—*The Australian*, August 11, 2003

Strange to live in New England and have an obsession about avoiding the "northeast corridor," the most dangerous, chronically-under-repair, and unpredictable highway in the country. Especially between Connecticut and New York. Yet June first of 2004, all phobias aside, found us taking just that route to Newark, New Jersey for an evening worship service in honor of the fifteenth anniversary of The OASIS, a justice ministry of the Episcopal Diocese of Newark that was started under Bishop John Spong. The OASIS is a "ministry of cultural and racial diversity with all who experience prejudice and oppression because of their sexual orientation or expression." Pat had spent several years trying to convince the bishops in Connecticut to allow her to create an OASIS ministry here, with no luck despite great support and encouragement from the people in Newark, including the current bishop. The guest preacher at the service that June 1st was Bishop Gene Robinson, who thirty-one years ago in that same church, had been the only openly-gay priest in the *country.*

We left hours in advance, knowing the kinds of traffic nightmares that could bring us to a stand-still on either I-95 or the Merritt Parkway. We chose the latter and drove along smoothly until just before the Tappan Zee bridge, where traffic began to crawl. We inched across the bridge and traveled what seemed, at that speed, like endless miles to the exit for the Garden State Parkway. Taking the Parkway exit at last, our relief was short-lived when we saw thousands of cars in bumper-to-bumper traffic. As we inched into our lane the wind picked up and rain started to fall, pelting the immobilized mass of vehicles. The sky turned black. The rain became a deluge and we figured the gig was up. We knew our exit was only a few miles away, but at this rate we wouldn't be there for another three days. The sound of the storm changed, and the pelting became a hailstorm coming out of the sky and piling up in such amounts that it looked as though snow banks had formed on the sides of the road. Miraculously, traffic started to move just as we were wondering if snowplows would be needed and we saw what the greater problem had been: ahead of us, the storm water was rushing in strong currents, flooding whole sections of the road and washing out the shoulders. Road debris was scattered randomly as cars narrowed to a single lane, picking their way through the mess one vehicle at a time.

We forged the flooding and the storm subsided. The sun came out, and the whole world sparkled in the evening light as we pulled into the church parking lot with ten minutes to spare and just behind a tornado that had touched down nearby. Through the window I could see Gene Robinson (the man who says his agenda is to be a "good bishop, not a gay bishop"[42]) in his crimson robe lining up with the other clergy.

This was an Episcopal church, but we were surrounded by openly-gay people as we took our seats. African drummers started to play and the "Entrance Rite" began. The pipe organ joined the drumming, which created a mesmerizing, other-worldly affect as the clergy proceeded up the center aisle. We sang—and our voices were strong, celebrative—a sound that could have lifted the rafters. Rare in Episcopal churches.

When it came time for the sermon and the microphone didn't work, Bishop Robinson laughed and said, "That's OK, I'll just speak loudly. I've been through much worse than this in the last year!" The sermon was about Pentecost, which we had clearly just driven through: "This is the time of Pentecost," he said, "the craziest, wildest season of the church year, for there is an element of danger in letting the Holy Spirit into your life," he said. "This Spirit will not be contained; it will be on its own and unpredictable like the wind. Everything that has been nailed down will come loose, and the whole earth will see and know that the things which were cast down are being raised up:

When the Day of Pentecost had come, they were all together in one place. And suddenly from Heaven there came a sound like the rush of a violent wind, and it filled the entire house where they were sitting . . . a violent wind . . . The kind of wind that uproots trees, turns over homes, and fills women and men with awe.

—Acts 2: 1-11

He talked about the winds of change, and how far we have come in the last fifteen years; and he advised gay Christians to reclaim scripture, "for what is Exodus," he said, "but the story of each of our 'coming out?'"

As Pat and I held hands in an Episcopal church filled to overflowing with gay people and their supporters, we watched Gene Robinson, the man who says the "H" word is for "honesty," not "homosexuality."[43] He looked radiant and at peace; he looked joyful, loving and wise; he exuded everything I would want or expect from a bishop. His entire presentation stood in direct contrast to the people who would have kept him down, his "sisters and brothers in Christ," the "God Hates Fags"—aligned religious fundamentalists who spout "the word of God" from faces contorted with hatred and rage.

At the reception afterward Pat asked the bishop how this last year has been for him. "It's been wonderful," he said as his infectious joy filled the room. "I know there are many people who don't want me to be happy, but this has been the happiest year of my life!"

Gene Robinson made only one personal comment on the gay issue, and it was this: "I have still to meet the married couple whose marriage is undermined by my commitment to my partner."

Amen, brother.

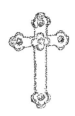

Between One Man and One Woman

The Vatican on Thursday vigorously condemned gay mar-
riage and urged lawmakers around the world—Catholic
and non-Catholic alike—to defend the 'common good' of
society by fighting the legalization of same-sex union.
Hoping to halt what it called an alarming trend, the
Vatican urged politicians to join in the struggle to pre-
serve traditional marriages between men and women and
prohibit homosexuals from adopting children. 'Homo-
sexual relationships are immoral and deviant, and only
traditional marriages can fulfill God's plan for the repro-
duction of the human race,' the Vatican said . . .

—*The Los Angeles Times*, August 1, 2003

President Bush said today that while he believed Ameri-
cans should treat gays in a welcoming and respectful man-
ner, he remained firmly opposed to gay marriages and
that administration lawyers were working to ensure that
the term 'marriage' would cover only unions between men
and women.

—*The New York Times*, July 31, 2003)

"The year 2003 will likely be remembered as one of the most significant years in the struggle for gay civil rights," wrote Anne Stanback, President of *Love Makes a Family*, on December 30th of that year: "In early June, the highest court of Ontario, Canada ruled that same-sex couples could not be barred from marriage. Within weeks, hundreds of couples from both Canada and the United

States were legally married in North America for the first time. Not to be outdone, the U.S. Supreme Court made its own stand for the equality of its gay and lesbian citizens in the landmark Lawrence v. Texas ruling. This eloquent decision overturned the existing sodomy laws in this country and established a significant precedent that gays and lesbians are indeed covered under the Constitution's equal protection clause."

The predictable conservative response began by the end of that month when, echoing Sen. Rick Santorum's linkage of gays to bestiality and incest, Senate Republican Leader Bill Frist (R-TN) "declared all-out war on gay Americans by endorsing an amendment to the U.S. constitution that would ban gay marriage." He told ABC's "This Week" that he feared the Supreme Court's decision declaring anti-gay sodomy laws unconstitutional could open people's homes to "prostitution" and "illegal commercial drug activity."[44]

Yet on November 18th of 2003 the Supreme Judicial Court of Massachusetts ruled that same-sex couples have a Constitutional right to marry, prompting Anne Stanback to predict that "we are likely to soon see the most significant backlash against gay, lesbian, bisexual and transgender people in our nation's history."

The year 2004 hasn't been any less intense. History was made on February 13th at 11:06 a.m. when the mayor of San Francisco took matters into his own hands and issued a marriage license to the first same-sex couple to be officially married in the United States. That first license, followed by thousands of others as gay couples lined the streets waiting for their turn at town hall, was issued to lesbians Del Martin and Phyllis Lyon who had been together for *fifty-one years*. It was August before the California Supreme Court annulled those 4,000 San Francisco gay marriages, saying that the mayor had overstepped his authority. On May 17th of 2004, however, Massachusetts, the Commonwealth that gave us American independence, became the first state to issue marriage licenses to same-sex couples. Gay couples in Cambridge started gathering for marriage licenses right after midnight the night of the 16th as President George W. Bush vowed to renew his efforts to amend the United States Constitution to make these marriages illegal. At the same time three bishops who had *supported* gay marriage in the Episcopal Diocese of Massachusetts apparently changed their minds and, citing their allegiance to their national denomination (the Episcopal Church USA and the global Anglican Communion) concluded that there is no room for same-sex marriage under church law. "Holy Matrimony," according to the church's constitution and canons, "is physical and spiritual union of a man and a woman.'[45] The Episcopal Diocese of Massachusetts is barring its priests from officiating at same-sex weddings, citing restrictive language in the canons and prayer book of the church . . .The prohibition, in a state where hundreds of clergy have said they support same-sex marriage, is setting up serious conflict and the possibility of ecclesiastical trials within several major denominations, wrote Michael Paulson in *The Boston Globe*.[46]

Three steps forward; two steps back. And the struggle goes on. By the end of August, an advocacy group for same-sex marriage was calling on gays and lesbians to stage a one-day nation-wide economic "walkout" on October 8th called "Walkout For Equality." On that day, GLBT Americans and their straight allies should not purchase anything, not generate sales tax or business revenue, not work, and not use cell phones. Estimates indicate that America's lesbian and gay population spends an average of $1.4 billion each day, totaling $500 billion each year. The walkout would make that point clear, highlighting the contributions that lesbians and gays make to the domestic economy and tax base, at the same time they are denied the full protections and civil liberties afforded heterosexual America. The Atlanta-based Boycott for Equality was inspired by Don't Amend founder Robin Tyler's famous quip, "If being gay is a disease, let's all call in sick to work!"[47]

"We are portrayed as these weird, deviant, sex-crazed people," says Therese Stewart, the deputy city attorney who leads San Francisco's gay-marriage litigation, "When in fact what most people are starting to realize is that we're pretty much as boring as everyone else!"[48] Jim McGreevey's resignation as governor of New Jersey and his admission that he is a "gay American" prompted columnist Arianna Huffington to write, *What if the world were a more welcoming place where gay people could have in their lives all the 'good things' and all the 'right things' without having to pretend they're straight? . . . So until the final curtain falls, let's seize the moment to reaffirm, loudly and without reservation, that to be gay is to be normal—whether you're a governor or a gardener, a public figure or a very private one.*[49]

Preach it, sister.

If Assholes Were Airplanes . .

Despite Christian injunctions about the equality of all human beings, it took centuries for the Church to recognize that scriptural endorsements of slavery were unsound . . . The Bible was used to justify apartheid in South Africa. The Church for hundreds of years condemned the ideas of human rights and democracy. Until recently, The Bible was used to approve second-class status for the gender whom St. Paul told to remain silent in church . . .

—*The Independent* (London), October 16, 2003

Around the world in the last few years, just when I started to care, the press has offered the reading public interviews, articles, and editorials that portray the "homosexual issue" in relation to the church as exactly the circus it has become and better than I could have begun to put into words. This is one of my favorites, taken from *Bigotry and the Bishops*, by Richard Holloway (former bishop of Edinburgh, Scotland and author of *Godless Morality*) and published in *The Guardian* on June 28, 2003:

Question: when is a homophobe not a bigot?
Answer: when he is motivated by sincere religious convictions.

That is now official doctrine in the Church of England . . . it's the Bible that is the problem. Christians believe that the Bible is inspired by God, though they mean different things by the claim. Some believe that God dictated every syllable, so nothing may be questioned or deviated from. Others believe that God inspired human beings to write it, thereby allowing for errors to creep in.

It would be easier to live with either doctrine if the specific scriptures stuck to giving us information about God that was otherwise unavailable. Unfortunately, they also contain a lot of specific directions on how human beings are to live, something about which we have a lot of knowledge and experience.

Everything is alright when the Bible sticks to generalities, such as loving your neighbor and being kind to strangers. The difficulty comes when it gets into details about human relations. Given its age and provenance, this is hardly surprising. The Old Testament reflects the way things were done by a Bedouin tribe 3,000 years ago. The New Testament reflects the attitudes of a splinter group a thousand years later, who believed that God had sent his agent to announce the end of the world—and since he would be coming back soon to wind everything up, there was not much point in getting too settled.

Theologians have found subtle ways of adapting these ancient obscurities to contemporary needs. One of their ruses is to make a distinction between the ethical and the metaphysical: the ethics of the Bible reflect its historical origins and can be reinterpreted; the metaphysics reflect eternal truth that cannot be tampered with.

Thus, the subordination of women to men and the prohibition on divorce—both clearly stated in scripture—can be modified to adapt the church to contemporary society; but the doctrine of the Trinity remains sacrosanct because it reflects the unchanging nature of God, not the flux of human history.

But we run up against a mysterious roadblock when we try to apply this sensible interpretative division to homosexuality. That bit is apparently still commanded by God, though he has let us off discriminating against women and condemning the divorced to lifelong celibacy.

Why is the conviction so solid here, when it proved so flexible in the other two areas? Given that there's hardly anything about homosexuality in the Bible, but a great deal about the subordination of women, the conclusion has to be that there is something atavistic going on here—straightforward bigotry.

That's why the fact should be proclaimed from the rooftops that the church in this country is the last bastion of legalized homophobia . . . At the end of the ugly debate on homosexuality at the 1998 Lambeth conference, Barbara Harris, the first woman bishop in the Anglican communion, was heard to mutter: 'If assholes were airplanes, this conference would be an airport.'

Leaving the Parish

We grow up with an outsider's perspective on mainstream society: it gives us a certain objectivity about the business of ordinary life, and a special sensitivity towards people who are struggling or feeling like outsiders themselves. We have generally done plenty of soul-searching, and been through some process of self-doubt and then redemption. We know who we are, we know what it is to be fully human, we know what it is to discover love, we know that love is costly, and we know what it is to know God and have our lives transformed—and we seek to share God's compassion in a needy world. And so to find some calm at the eye of the storm, and get on with the week ahead . . .

—Anonymous Gay Vicar from Northern England

As Pat continued to mature, once more her questions deepened. She *had* done plenty of soul-searching, and she *had* moved right through the heart of self-doubt to redemption. As she came out on the other side and felt what it is to be fully human, to discover love, and to know what it is to have her life transformed, she began to chafe under the restrictions of the Episcopal Church, especially as it relates to homosexuals. She found she could no longer keep herself squeezed into the box created by dogma and creed, the tiny world created by giving one's power over to the "outside authority" of an institution built by men to tell her how to experience God. She *knew* what it was to know God, and for all intents and purposes, it was nothing like the Church's version of "Him." She *knew* what it was to be an outcast (as Jesus was), and to have people refuse to attend church or refuse to serve on the altar with her because she is homosexual; she was tired of trying to work within an institution which was still debating whether or not she has the right to be included in the full "body of Christ;" a Church more interested in her sexual orientation than the success of her ministry. Furthermore, she was tired of the patriarchal language, the church hierarchy, and the "old boy network." She was tired of offering to be proactive for homosexuals within the church in as many ways as she could (because she *does* have "a special sensitivity towards people who are struggling or feeling like outsiders themselves"), only to be met with polite smiles and false words of encouragement. Above all, she was tired of presiding over the kind of congregation that tied itself in knots when her photograph appeared on the front page of the religion section of the local newspaper as a supporter of gay rights. "We don't want to be a 'poster church' for gay rights," the people had said.

Pat's calling, which has *always* been "to seek to share God's compassion in a needy world" no longer matched with what the Church was doing to "compassion" in God's name. The days when she came alive as a parish priest were over. Her idealistic hope to be a catalyst for gay rights within her diocese had faded in the face of closed doors and constipated rhetoric. The Church which had, through her entire life, filled her with light, enthusiasm, and love for others—the place where she and her calling to serve God were one—had become so heavy and oppressive that it was beginning to feel like her heterosexual marriage. She could hardly breathe. It was time to re-evaluate.

She went on retreat to think this through. She wanted a revelation; she wanted answers; she wanted to know what to do. After three days of quiet at a large retreat center in Massachusetts, she had had enough of the strict regime of vegetarian food, no sugar and no caffeine, enough of the walking, reading and journal-writing that seemed to produce no real insights, enough of seeking answers that wouldn't come. She almost left to come home early, but forced herself to stay. On the fourth day she received what she had been waiting for—she heard God talking to her:

"What do I need to do for my next step? How do I prepare?," she asked.

Do not fear, Patricia, there are angels and guides all around you. You will know what to do. Stay the road; they will guide you. Look for them in the wisdom of others, in the books you pick up, in the seeds you scatter, and in the hearts you hear speak, she heard back.

"Will it be soon?," she asked.

Now. It is now. Drop all, leave all, and as I've said to you before, come follow me, came the answer.

"Who are you now? Are you the God I've known in the past?" she asked.

Are you the Patricia you've known in the past? came the reply.

"No," she said.

Then no, she heard.

"But aren't you the same, now, forever, and always?" she asked.

Are you the same, now, forever, and always? she heard.

"No," she answered.

Then, no! came the response.

"So as I change, you change?" she asked.

Yes. I change to allow you to grow in me. As you grow, your divinity stretches within you. Your divine self gets to look more and more like me. And all kinds of mysteries open up to you and you step forward. And you go on, was the answer.

"But I am having trouble naming you now. Why is that?" she asked.

I have expanded. You are in a place of transition. And I, as well as you, must wait for what you will call me. Or what you will not *call me!* she heard.

"I'm so confused. All my life I have thought I was a Christian. And now, now I'm not sure what I am. Do you know what I am?" she asked.

Ah yes, my Patricia. You are my dreams taken flesh, my alpha and omega of Patricias. You are the compassionate heart of a woman born to set the oppressed and broken-hearted free. I have allowed you your pain so that your heart could break open again and find its way out; its way home to me. I know you can understand what I am saying even though your pain is still with you, she heard in response. . .

"So will my heart ever be . . . Never mind, I know," she said.

"Drop all, leave all . . . and come follow me." She had heard this before, and it always took her on a straight course to the bottom line. She knew what she had to do. The month was May. She called the diocese and said that she would be leaving her parish by the end of the summer. A deep sadness settled upon her. "For the first time," she told me, "I feel old." "I've known all my life that I was born to be a priest, and for the first time, I'm not sure what that means. What I *do* know as a homosexual is that *our time is now.* Outside of conservative parish life there is a big wide world where my sexual orientation can be an attribute, not a det-riment, and *that's* where I'm going to live.

The Sanctuary

I thank you God for this most amazing day;
for the leaping greenly spirits of trees
and a blue true dream of sky; and for everything
which is natural, which is infinite, which is yes

— e. e. cummings

Emerald is the word most people use to describe the green of the Sanctuary's new spring grass as it fills the lawn and fields that surround us. This is New England. We spend our winters trying to survive the darkness, bitter cold and snow or, if not, ice. When spring arrives, always at least a month after we feel entitled to it, we burst out of hibernation, "leaping greenly spirits" indeed, to bask in air that has no bite and sun that doesn't yet burn.

Pat and I live in paradise, if the truth be known, on forty acres of "pristine Connecticut countryside," as the brochure now says, land given to her years before we met, to use "for the glory of God." She wasn't free to use it at all until we came together, and then, a vision she had held for over twenty years became a reality. For much of her life Pat had told everyone who would listen that she wanted someday to build a retreat center in which to live and from which to minister to others. The over-arching problem was that it wasn't going to happen—even after she had been given the property on which to do it—until she came into "right relationship" with herself. From *there* she could create, and from *there* she could minister to others.

By the time we had each divested ourselves of worldly possessions and moved to East Haddam, the little house on the Sanctuary property, which hadn't been used in over a decade, was crumbling and the land was almost impassable. Dead trees and their tangled branches, vines of every description, poison ivy so thick it was dangerous just to breathe the air, and scrub brush and bramble harboring rusted barbed wire, broken bottles, rotting fences, and pieces of old shacks were much of what one saw coming into the driveway. "Driveway," in fact, is a stretch.

The house could barely be seen from the road, and the little storage shed couldn't be seen from the house. There were no parking areas; visitors in those days often had to be pushed back out to the street after they had gotten stuck in the mud.

It took a slew of passionate friends with a vast array of abilities and areas of enthusiasm, as well as the passionate people they brought with them, six months to renovate the house and clear the land. In the process we used up a mountain of shovels, picks, clippers, chain saws, power tools, lawn mowers and other machines whose remains eventually made quite a mark on the town dump. We worked with intention; we wrote prayers and inserted them into new walls and cement pilings. We created "sacred space," welcoming space, a place of hospitality, a safe place for seekers (especially those wounded by a homophobic society) where wisdom can be found and the mystery of the divine explored, whether it happens by "coming out" or "going within."

People often hear about us long before we know who they are, and despite initial growing pains and the maturing process of learning how to manage what we have set out to do, from its inception, this small spiritual life center with a special ministry to the gay community has already brought people together from all walks of life, races, cultures, religious and spiritual traditions, and sexual orientation whose paths might otherwise never have crossed. The Sanctuary hosts adults who bring their friends and partners, grandparents who bring their grandchildren, teenagers who bring other teens, children who bring their parents, and neighbors who bring their guests. Gay couples, straight couples, and inter-racial couples have celebrated their unions on this land.

Pat is not an "animal person," so we only have two goats, two dogs and a cat. We keep bees (for environmental purposes so they don't count as pets) and are hosting a *bee school* that will eventually produce Sanctuary honey and beeswax candles. We make soap that is blessed, wrapped, and sold by a group called ACTS (Active Contemplatives of The Sanctuary) whose mission statement includes the words "To seek community, tranquility, and harmony . . . embracing meditation, discussion, and prayer, we will work together to honor the land around us and create legacies for future seekers . . ." A variety of people bring "their people" to the Sanctuary for workshops and retreats, and they come with new ideas for reaching out to others who could join us. Neighbors fill out our landscaping projects with cuttings from their gardens; the town sends truckloads of mulch and wood chips simply because we ask; and meetings of a local conservation group dedicated to claiming and protecting the town's scenic sites and "open spaces" are held in the Sanctuary's "yurt."

The Sanctuary can be quiet (discounting the owls and geese, the bull frogs and wild turkey, the coyotes and birds that surround us), or bursting with celebration; it can be solitary, or filled with community. It is where I hope, finally, to make a small mark on the world toward the good, for at the end of the day when the rare red-headed woodpecker and the great blue heron are still safe in their wetlands home that abuts our ponds, the Baltimore Oriole has sung itself to a parade rest in the apple tree, the bees and goats have been fed, I've rescued a baby snapping turtle from the cat and negotiated with a family of snakes for access to the berry patch (You can nest again next spring under the tarps if you give me the summer), the Sanctuary is a place where I am constitutionally happy for the first time in my life. It is a place "which is natural, which is infinite, which is yes!"

Labyrinth
(for Mattie)

We need to stop.
Just stop.
Stop for a moment . . .
Before anybody
Says or does anything
That may hurt anyone else.
We need to be silent.
Just silent.
Silent for a moment . . .
Before we forever lose
The blessing of songs
That grow in our hearts. . .

—Mattie Stepanek, "Our World" in *Hope Through Heartsongs*

The labyrinth is the first thing I see when I open the door in the morning. It's in the field at a distance from the house, but its pattern is magnetic. It draws the eye. As does the form of a lone Canadian goose unfolding its head from under a wing at sunrise right at the center. Later, a mammoth wild turkey struts around the perimeter for an hour with its tail feathers fanned to display his magnificence, and by noon, the orange cat will also seek the labyrinth's center to sun himself on the large rock where people often sit. That center rock was the only place of "higher ground" we could initially find in the otherwise flat field when it was a tangle of tall grass, vines, prickly plants and thistle. We stumbled upon it during one of the first forays from the house toward the woods and climbed up to be high enough to see where we had been and where we were going. Looking at where we have been and toward where we might be going is a good *reason* to step out of the absurdity, chaos and confusion that can (at the low points, especially if you are a gay priest in today's church, for example) constitute daily life.

Labyrinths allow us to move out of linear reality. They have been used as a sacred symbol and a means for meditation and prayer for thousands of years, although their origin is unknown. They can be found at sacred sites throughout the world, for encoded in the complex geometric pattern are forms of ancient wisdom that take one to deeper spiritual realities and lead to the "prayerful inner depths of the heart."

> *We need to notice.*
> *Just notice.*
> *Notice for a moment . . .*
> *Before the future slips away*
> *Into ashes and dust of humility . . .* [50]

In the Christian tradition labyrinths came into being around the 13th century and were used by pilgrims to replace the literal journey to Jerusalem and the Holy Land. Christian pilgrims walked a symbolic journey to Jerusalem, following the footsteps of Jesus.

Walking a labyrinth, which combines the circle and the spiral into a path with one way in and one way out, can be a metaphor for life. "You can't really tell where you're going, and you can see only part of where you've been," says an article about a labrynth used as part of a University of Maine summer course. "Stress seems to melt away as you wander the short, twisted path, and just when you think you've finished, you realize you're not even close. By the time you reach the middle, a transformation has taken place. You're centered, focused, calm."[51]

Or the walk toward the labyrinth's center can be a symbolic "descent into life's dark mysteries," and the walk back out, "a 'rebirth' into a second life of wisdom and understanding.[52]

However it is done, a labyrinth walk is a pilgrimage.

"I walked not sure of my turns or where I was going, yes to the center, but that's all I knew," wrote one Sanctuary labyrinth walker. "At the center I prayed a good prayer, not the formal ones I know," she wrote. "I took a journey and had a pressing feeling that the walk in was an uphill journey, but the way out became down hill. All too ironic seeing as the landscape is the opposite," wrote another. "The curves, the turns, the paths that lead back against themselves ultimately take me to where I was meant to be," says an anonymous entry in the Sanctuary's labyrinth journal.

———————

I have yet to "walk" the labyrinth on my knees, but someday I will. This thought has been with me since the hot afternoon I followed closely behind our engineer friend with the lawn mower as he marked the labyrinth pattern and I cut the path. Part of the labyrinth's great power is that it forces one to slow down. Like conscious breathing and writing with the non-dominant hand, slowing down is sometimes all it takes to find inner wisdom. *The slower I walked, the better I felt*, I wrote after my first labyrinth experience. *Like the pressure of having to do it all quickly and effi-ciently had melted away . . .*

> *We need to be.*
> *Just be.*
> *Be for a moment . . .*
> *Kind and gentle, innocent and*
> *Trusting.*
> *Like children and lambs,*
> *Never judging or vengeful*
> *Like the judging and vengeful.*
> *And now, let us pray.*
> *Differently, yet together,*
> *Before there is no earth, no life,*
> *No chance for peace.*[53]

Mattie Stepanek began writing poetry at the age of three in response to the death of one of his brothers. Confined to a wheel-chair and on full life support whereever he went, Mattie suffered from dysautonomic mitochondrial myopathy, a genetic disorder and rare form of muscular dystropy which took the lives of his three older siblings. Doctors don't know why Mattie didn't die at birth, or why he lived as long as he did. His name, Matthew, means "gift from God," and he believed that God allowed him to live to spread his message of peace and hope to the world through the inner voice he called a "heartsong." Mattie died on June 22, 2004, the author of five best-selling books of poetry. He was thir-teen years old.

Turning the Corner

The dawn of the twenty-first century is a crossroads for the human race. We are living at a time of both intensified fear and intensified love, both encroaching barbarism and spiritual renaissance. Our consciousness now is backed by so much material power that, whether it is attuned to fear or attuned to love affects the future of the entire human race.

—Marianne Williamson, *Healing the Soul of America*

I began my fiftieth year in August of 2003, just as we were able to see with the naked eye—for the last time in any of our lives—the planet Mars. There it was, named for the Roman God of war, glowing fiery red in the night sky over planet Earth whose inhabitants are, to this day, consumed with violence and war.

Our world is in desperate ecological and spiritual straights according to all reliable accounts. And yet there are subtle and growing signs that the sluggish collective human consciousness is finally realizing it has no choice but to wake up if we are to have any future at all. There is hope, I believe—all superficial evidence to the contrary.

Perhaps at this crossroad we are ready to turn the corner to the next stage of evolution, to an "emerging paradigm," a new way of seeing the whole.[54] If nothing else, as the world becomes smaller and geography no longer divides us, the fact that we are *one* human race, sisters and brothers, bound forever by the common denominator of needing to breathe in, and breathe out in order to survive, becomes strikingly obvious. If we really *are* one, how pointless it becomes to kill, torture, maim, or slander another.

Imagine if we were no longer susceptible to the message by every current instrument of governmental voice, that we must remain, at all costs, *afraid*, and therefore prepared to do violence to "protect" ourselves! Imagine, if at long last our arrogant, elitist, dominance-based "God-is-on-our-side" American "way" in the world had begun to run its course. Imagine an end to the macho, testosterone-driven "how dare they do that to us! We'll get the bastards! Slit their throats! Torture their citizens! Bomb their cities! Kill their women and children! and Show 'em who's boss" approach to taking the moral high ground which ensures the disgust of the rest of the world and our victims' thirst for revenge. Imagine, if we could show the world "the true nature and heart of America," as the President repeatedly calls it, without murdering anyone![55]

I am a gay person. I understand feelings of violence. There is as much murderous rage within me as there is in the people who horrify me. *Yet, violence can never stop violence because its very success leads others to imitate it. Paradoxically, violence is most dangerous when it succeeds . . .You cannot free people from the Domination System by using its own methods. You cannot construct the City of Life with weapons of death. You cannot make peace—real peace—with war.[56]*

———

Are we ready to put down our lethal toys and stop the "encroaching barbarism?" Are we courageous enough, finally, to explore the concept of living in a world not ordered by who will oppress whom? Can we *stop talking so much about 'war,' and reconcile ourselves to the fact that the punishment of terrorist crime and the gradual reduction of its threat cannot be translated into the satisfying language of decisive and dramatic conquest?* asks the Archbishop of Canterbury, who was 200 yards from the World Trade Center on September 11, 2001 *. . . Can we, for God's sake, let go of the fantasies nurtured by the capacity for high-tech aerial assault? As if the first move in any modern conflict had to be precision bombing? . . .* (From *Writing in the Dust, Reflections on the 11th September and its Aftermath*).[57] Are we ready to come out of our misguided, modern-day patriarchal fog which honors brute force above all else?

"The Patriarchy," read a sign at a recent rally for gay rights, "always equals War, Control, and Oppression." In many ways, says author Andrew Harvey, the world has "gone *mad . . .*" We have an American president who has been nominated, along with British Prime Minister Tony Blair, for the Nobel Peace Prize "*for having dared to go to war . . .,*"[58] and who is trying to amend the US constitution to "protect the institution of marriage," and "the future of our country," by denying committed same-sex couples the right to marry. (*In a military industrial state,* explained an article adapted from a sermon given at an Episcopal church in Boston, *it is much easier to fret and fume over what is happening at the marriage altar than dismantle and redirect a violence-based economy.*[59]) The country's religious "right" is apoplectic over homosexuals coming out of the closet, rejecting church authority, and demanding equal rights with depressing regularity and faster than religious leaders can condemn them in the name of God. We, the general population, have allowed ourselves to be manipulated and deceived by a color chart of terror-alert levels and political lies; we are needlessly at war because we would rather call another empire "evil" than examine our own hearts. We have American troops in Iraq (indoctrinated to kill to the sound of rock music) and gay youth at home committing suicide at a rate three times the national average. We are a people fired up by the trappings of power, dominance, and raw brutality; a country detested around the world. *When we try to overcome evil with evil, we are not working for peace,* says Thich Nhat Hanh in *Living Buddha, Living Christ. If you say, 'Saddam Hussein is evil' . . . and if you use the same means he has been using, you are exactly like him. If we look deeply into the weapons, we see our own mind—sour prejudices, fears, and ignorance . . . to work for peace is to uproot war from ourselves . . . .*"[60] Can we turn the corner?

I can't say why I believe we can, but against all odds I feel the potential. Something is happening. We're bottoming out and there's nowhere to go but up. We have passionate, articulate people climbing out of twenty years of political apathy to work for change, authors, whistle-blowers and internet organizations willing to expose the truth about our country so publicly and loudly they can't be ignored, and an expansion of human awareness in some quarters that changes us all forever. We have new heroes who believe that we have the power "to accept the suffering, to refuse to pass it on to another, to forgive, to end the needless torment, and, most of all, to transmute evil into energy for the vitality of the whole."[61]

Miracles are happening in every realm. Let me tell you about ours. Britain's Royal Air Force is reportedly embarking on a gay recruitment drive![62], and here at home a retired Coast Guard Admiral and two retired Army Generals—the highest-ranking military officers ever to acknowledge being gay—recently came out of the closet and denounced the "Don't Ask, Don't Tell" policy as contrary to the military's core values and an affront to the dignity of homosexuals. They are encouraging other gays in the military to do the same.[63] Bishop Gene Robinson of the Episcopal Church was happy to confirm in June of 2004 that he hasn't received a death threat in six months, and slowly but surely, one state at a time, same-sex couples are becoming legally recognized through the institution of marriage. As Bishop John Spong said to Pat and me when we met with him privately, "The battle is over. You *will* be legally married, and your relationship *will* be blessed by the church." Then he embraced us both in a three-person hug and said, "This is a bishop's blessing."

On the home front, a grandchild watched Pat's daughter-in-law introduce me to friends at an outdoor potluck supper (to which we were invited without reservation, miracle number one). "Hi, I'm Karen Hunter," I said, shaking hands. The seven-year-old looked at me in confusion and said for all to hear, "You have to have the same last name as *us*; you're *family*!"

A week later, Pat and I took the younger grandchildren to the town beach where we were stopped at the entrance and told that we needed two beach passes, one for each adult in the car. "Tell them you're *married*," piped a little voice loudly from the back seat.

We've begun to spend holidays and special occasions with Pat's son and daughter-in-law and their children, which—for a long time—you couldn't have convinced us would ever happen. And the crowning event in our quest to normalize "us" in relation to "them" occurred, by our standards, the day we were invited to spend the night at their house and sleep together on the pull-out-couch in the middle of the living room, where we were likely to be joined by the children or the family dog at any time. Does normal get any better than that?

Pieces like these were falling into place faster than we could absorb them, when, for the first time in six years, Pat and her ex-husband found themselves under the same roof watching their children's children in a summer-camp theater performance along with the rest of the family. No one had a heart attack (sorrow). Or a stroke (anger). Civil words were spoken. The little ones sat indiscriminately on any of our laps. And the walls came tumbling down.

We attended a workshop a few years back in which we were instructed to write down the first two words that came into our minds, choose one, and write on it. The first word I wrote was "prayer." The second was "hope." I couldn't choose between them, and wondered if perhaps they are the same thing. "Why?" I wrote. "I don't know. I'm not religious in any traditional sense, so why do I pray? Or, why do I call it prayer?"

"It just happens," I wrote, "and the prayer feels connected to hope. Hope for what? The world? Hardly. Humanity? Not a chance. Hope that we will achieve a measure of peace and harmony in our lifetimes? Nope.

What is it, then, that I call prayer and which occurs consistently throughout my days and nights? When I lie in bed listening to the quiet of the land on which we live, a rush of gratitude fills my heart and I hear the prayer starting:

Thank you for this beautiful place.
Thank you for my beautiful partner.
May we be well, may we all be well.
May the misery of the world be lifted;
May we all find peace and comfort;
May we let go of violence, of judgment, of hatred, and especially of fear . . .

———————

On it goes, this rhythmic, chanting prayer. Where does it start? Where does it end? I don't know . . . perhaps with a hope I didn't know I had until I wrote the word "hope" next to the word "prayer" and couldn't separate them; a hope perhaps I didn't really *have* until we moved through the pain to the promise."

I believe we can turn the corner.

For the Glory of God

Strange this journey leading
In the end no where but here,
The path our breathing,
The road our blood.
Yet every step is needed to arrive
Where beauty inundates our veins,
Suffuses living flesh with darkened light.
No wonder we, so long the wanderers,
Can't see at first we're home . . .

—Thomas Yeomans, "Love Now" one of four "Soul Canticles" in *On Earth Alive*[64]

Rock wall day was scheduled for 7:30 a.m. one spring morning because that's when "the motorcycle contingent" would arrive. We set the clock early to be up in time to bake two large pans of banana and pumpkin bread and put on the coffee for the hungry travelers, and cringed at the thought of any poor neighbor trying to sleep late that morning as these machines roared down country roads en route to our quiet spiritual-life center. Most of our neighbors, however, tend horses, cattle, goats, chickens, roosters or llamas and are probably up with the sun. My daughter's college friends, the ones with the bikes, are a tight-knit group of "Outing Club" members who spend their free time rolling their kayaks in class-4 or-5 rapids, "belaying" one another up and down unspeakable heights and suspicious crevices, sailing on kites attached to skis or surf boards (as best as I can understand), and otherwise looking for danger in whatever form nature has it to offer. This was just before exam week at school but (oddly enough) these young adults were willing to overlook that to offer their skills and their strength for an entire Saturday of tame volunteer activity. They joined other Sanctuary volunteers and our *Secret Life of Stones* author and wall-building artist. The task before us was to lay the foundation of a new wall out by the street using the stones from a long-collapsed wall nearby. The "alpha males" in the college group, as my daughter referred to them, took fifteen minutes to sort themselves out as to who was in charge of their tasks, and we began. People found their roles: the muscle-bound men lifted and hauled, those with average strength or bad backs collected small filler ("heart") stones, those with a good eye and sense of design determined where rocks should be placed, and others filled water glasses, organized lunch, and ran for ice packs, hydrogen peroxide, gauze and lawn chairs for those about to collapse. Neighbors drove by all day and cheered us on.

This is the way it goes at The Sanctuary. We work as the weather and the seasons permit and our projects draw enthusiasts through all kinds of Sanctuary connections whose skills show us the technicolor range of human aptitude. Like our labyrinth project which took two summers to complete, this stone wall will be an unfolding event, tended by people who want to be a part of the land and a part of the community it will take to create the wall. There's no hurry; we're not going anywhere. We simply wait to see who comes and what they have to offer—and they always come.

"The glory of God" was the stipulation set forth when the property was given; the land must be used for the glory of God. For some strange reason we have never felt any confusion about what this means; I say "for some strange reason" in reference to me, because I would have been the *last* person to define "the glory of God" under any other circumstances. Some people have had strong opinions about what they thought we should do here, and they eventually left disappointed when the Sanctuary wasn't "Christian enough" for them, or business-oriented enough, or growing fast enough, or exclusively gay enough, or exclusively female enough. What it comes down to for us, now that I really think about it, is that the glory of God is about life—so we celebrate life! We have neighbors whose political beliefs are as far to the right as ours are to the left, but when we join forces to collect wood chips for our gardens or care for one another's animals (herding wayward cows, clipping goats' hooves, returning lost dogs), our opposing beliefs make absolutely no difference. There are Bible-thumping, "drop-kick-me-Jesus-through-the-goalpost-of-life"-brand religious fundamentalists who work with us shoulder-to-shoulder on local town issues and have probably convinced themselves that Pat and I are merely "housemates." Whatever works! People who call themselves Quakers, Mormons, shamans, Catholics, Baptists, atheists, war veterans and peace activists, high-church, low-church, and no-church, have all joined hands in prayer circles at the Sanctuary, and the house and grounds have been "fed" by so many hands we've lost count.

We take our mission seriously: "to provide a supportive environment where those who come can find peace and common ground." We protect this mission above all else for it is where our hearts are. There is only one question we ask before turning our attention in any direction and the question is not, "Is it good for us?" (or our friends, or even our families). The question we ask is, "Is it good for the Sanctuary?" Sanctuary land can never be sold and never "developed." Someday, if another charitable organization doesn't take it over, the property will become part of the East Haddam Land Trust to be kept as "open space." Whatever happens after our time, may the Sanctuary be remembered as a place well-used "for the Glory of God" by a gay priest and the woman who loved her.

Afterward

About the families. It's taken time and in some cases, even time hasn't worked. Pat has a grown son who still will have nothing to do with her and grandchildren she has never seen. This, her mind cannot understand and her heart will never accept. Anyone who has lost a child knows that the pain can't really be put into words, so I won't try to say more. She has another child, however, who treats us politely, and a third who has come full circle and embraces us both as though life has always been this way. We are aware, every day, that this is a miracle. With one daughter-in-law there is a new closeness that might not have occurred if she and Pat hadn't taken this journey together.

My intention was not to give the impression throughout this book that my children are good and Pat's children are not; our offspring grew up under very different circumstances and spheres of influence, and their attitudes simply reflect that. Mine grew up without church dogma, and knowing (from infancy) an openly-gay grandfather and his life partner; hers were raised under the authority of the Catholic Church with its repressive views on sexuality, and parents who abhorred the topic of homosexuality because to broach it would have exposed the terminal flaw in their marital relationship.

The point now, in our view, is that seven years have come and gone and we have lived to tell about them loud and clear. We bask in the warmth of those who love us, and forgive those who trespass against us (Pat better than I, but I'm working on it). We hope they do the same for us.

Our years together have already been full, painful, joyful years of growth, intimacy, honesty, great humor, and unshakeable commitment. And here we are, moving forward in an era filled with promise! May we be well, may we *all* be well . . .

> *Here, yes, here is home at last!*
> *we step across the threshold stone,*
> *alive as we have never been,*
> *yet somehow also knowing this was ours*
> *at every step along the way . . .*

—Thomas Yeomans, *Love Now*[65]

Footnotes

Baptism By Fire

[1]The Book of Common Prayer, p. 305, The Bishops, the Clergy, and the Laity of the Protestant Episcopal Church in the USA, 1789.

Here I Am, Lord

[2]The Book of Common Prayer, p. 531

[3]*Here I Am, Lord,* 1981. Daniel L. Schutte, S.J. and NALR, 10802 N. 23rd Ave., Phoenix. AZ 85029

If We Could Hold Hands Around the World

[4] Adapted from *Spiritual Notes to Myself*, Hugh Prather, p. 137, Conari Press, Berkeley, CA, 1998

[5]"The Wine and the Cup" in *Teachings of Rumi*, Andrew Harvey, p. 3, Shambahala Publications, Inc. 1999

Coming Out

[6]*Virtually Normal,* Andrew Sullivan, p 191.

The Bread of Heaven . . .

[7]*A World Lit Only By Fire*, William Manchester, p.27, Little, Brown and Company, 1992, 1993

[8]*Jesus What He Really Said and Did*, Stephen Mitchell, pp. xix-xxi, HarperCollins Publishers, NY, 2002

[9]*Why Christianity Must Change or Die*, John Shelby Spong, p.4 HarperCollins Publishers, NY, 1998

[10]*Here I Stand*, John Shelby Spong, pp. 242-243, HarperCollins Publishers, Inc., NY, 2001

[11]*Love and Doubts. What is Left of Christianity*, Richard Holloway, p. 13, Canongate Books, Ltd., Edinburgh, Scotland, 2001

[12]From a talk given by Andrew Harvey at The Hartford Seminary, October 2003

[13]*The Heart of Christianity*, Marcus J. Borg, pp. 7, 13, 14, HarperSanFrancisco, A Division of HarperCollins Publishers, 1989.

[14]*Here I Stand*, p. 244

[15] *Love and Doubts*, p. 32

[16] From "The Holy Eucharist, Rite Two," The Common Book of Prayer, p. 355

[17] From a lecture at the United States Coast Guard Academy, Cindy Lee VanDover, College of William and Mary, March, 2003

Contrasts

[18] Rev. Ray Jones, Jr., pastor, Lighthouse Community Baptist Church, Op Ed page, *The Day* (New London, CT)

[19] Rev. Samuel R. Williams, Rector of St. Albans Episcopal Church in McCook, NE, *The McCook Gazette* (McCook, NE), August 8, 2003. editor@mccookgazette.com

The MCC Fellowship

[20] *The Lord is My Shepherd. and He Knows I'm Gay*, Rev. Troy D. Perry, p. 132, Universal Fellowship Press, Los Angeles, CA, 1972

[21] Ibid, pp. 139-140

Gay Youth

[22] "Suicide & Homosexual Teens." Mike V. Smith & Mary Drake, March 1, 2001, GLSEN library (www.GLSEN.org)

[23] Children of the Shadows was an organization that is now called True Colors, Inc. Sexual Minority Youth and Family Services. This not-for-profit organization works to eliminate the stigma associated with sexual and gender minority status and to ensure that the needs of lesbian, gay, bi-sexual, transgendered, intersex and other sexual minorities are completely met by those responsible for their education, health, and well-being.

Sexuality

[24] *Born of A Woman*, John Shelby Spong, pp. 215-216, HarperCollins Publishers, NY, 1992

[25] *The Soul of Sex*, by Thomas Moore, p. xii, HarperCollins Publishers, NY, 1998

[26] *Coming Out Spiritually*, p. 99

[27] *The Man Jesus Loved,* Theodore W. Jennings, Jr., pp. 86-87, The Pilgrim Press, Cleveland, OH, 2003

[28] *The Soul of Sex*, p. xiii

May We Pray With You

29 From Plowshare Peace and Justice Center website: http://
www.plowshare.org/plowshare.htm

30 *The Hartford Courant,* October 18, 1998

Homosexuality and the Bible

31 *We Were Baptized Too*, pp xvii-xviii

32 "Homosexuality and the Bible," by Walter Wink, p. 14 (pamphlet)

The Archbishop of Canterbury

33 Episcopal News Service, 23 July 2002—182, website:http://
episcopalchurch.org/ens/202-182.html

34 The Ananova News Service, UIC, Feb. 26, 2003

35 *The Atlanta Journal and Constitution,* Oct. 16, 2003

36 *The Daily Telegraph,* May 14, 2003

37 *The Reading Evening Post,* July 1, 2003

38 Ibid

39 *The Independent*, London, Oct. 16, 2003

40 *The Guardian*, July 8, 2003

41 America Online: LBJ3761, Dec. 19, 2003

Gene Robinson

42 *TheAustralian,* August 11, 2003

43 Ibid

Between One Man and One Woman

44 John Aravosis, *The List*, June 30, 2003 http://hatecrime.org/
support.html

45 "The Boston Globe," may 13, 2004

46 Ibid

47 "Gay Marriage Group Calls National Boycott," by 365 Gay.com
Newsletter staff, Aug. 25, 2004 8:32 pm ET

48 *USA Today,* March 22, 2004

49 Arianna Online, Aug. 13, 2004, "Jim McGreevey: 'I Am A Gay
American. ' "

Labyrinth

[50]"Our World" in *Hope Through Heartsongs,* Mattie Stepanek, quoted in "Science of Mind Magazine," April 2004, p, 14.

[51]*The Bangor Daily News,* Sept. 8, 200,

[52]*Utne Reader,* Jan-Feb, 1998, p. 84

[53]"Our World," Mattie Stepanek

Turning the Corner

[54]*The Heart of Christianity,* p. 4

[55]*The New York Times,* Friday, May 7, 2004

[56]*Engaging the Powers,* Walter Wink, p. 216, Augsburg Fortress, Minneapolis, MN, 1992

[57]*Writing in the Dust: Reflections on the I I th September and its Aftermath.* by Rowan Williams, pp. 49-51, Hodder and Stoughton, A Division of Hodder Headline Ltd, London, 2002

[58]Yahoo News, Feb. 1, 2004: "Bush, Blair and EU nominated for Nobel Peace Prize as deadline closes, " http:story.news.yahoo.com/news?tmpl=story&u=/afp/20040201/wl_uk_afp/nobel_peace_0...

[59]*Kicking the Dog,* William Blaine-Wallace, adapted from a sermon delivered on June 27, 2004 at Emmanuel Episcopal Church in Boston, MA, centered on the gospel reading of Luke 9:51-62, received from People of Faith for Gay Civil Rights,http://www.pfgcr.org/warandgays.html

[60]*Living Buddha. Living Christ,* Thich Nhat Hanh, pp. 75,76, Riverhead Books, a division of G.P. Putnam and Sons, NY, 1995

[61]*The Universe is a Green Dragon,* Brian Swimme, p. 81, Bear and Company, Inc., Sante Fe, NM, 1984

[62]365Gay.com Newscenter staff, August 30, 2004

[63]Crusaders—Military Secrets , *People Magazine,* January 12, 2004, p. 155.

For the Glory of God

[64]*"Love Now,"* one of four Soul Canticles in *On Earth Alive,* Thomas Yeomans, Morningstar Press, Concord, MA 2000. Reprinted by permission of the author.

Afterward

[65]*Ibid*

The Sanctuary

The Sanctuary at Shepardfields, Inc. is a not-for-profit, tax-exempt, 501 (c) (3) organization located at 59 Bogel Road, East Haddam, CT 06423. Proceeds from the sale of this book will be used to support the Sanctuary and its mission. For more information, please visit the website at:

www.shepardfields.org

or call the Sanctuary at 860-873-9904.